Read On 1

BEGINNING

Nancy Nici Mare

McGraw-Hill Contemporary

James Chang

For Joseph, Elizabeth, and Steven.

The publisher would like to thank the following for their permission to reproduce photographs:
Cover Photo Credits: © Louis Ducharme, © Shaun Walker, © Electrolux, © Steve Kaufman/CORBIS
Interior Photo Credits: p. 2 © Twinstuff, p. 6 © Craig Cunningham, p. 12 © Catherine Karnow/CORBIS,
p. 16 © Strauss/Curtis/CORBIS, p. 22 © Jose Luis Pelaez, Inc./CORBIS, p. 26 © Michael Barley/CORBIS,
p. 32 © Jon Feingersh/CORBIS, p. 36 © LWA-Dann Tardif/CORBIS, p. 42 © Ronnie Kaufman/CORBIS,
p. 46 photo on left © AP Wide World Photo, p. 46 photo on right © Erik S. Lesser, p. 52 © Louis Ducharme,
p. 56 © Steve Kaufman/CORBIS, p. 62 © Galen Rowell/CORBIS, p. 66 © Shaun Walker, p. 72 © James
Marshall/CORBIS, p. 76 © Philip Game, p. 82 © Electrolux, p. 86 photo on left © Ryan McVay, photos on
right © Ryan McVay, © Royalty Free/CORBIS, p. 92 photo on left © Bettmann/CORBIS, p. 92 photo on
right © Bettmann/CORBIS, p. 96 © George Waymire

Read On 1, First Edition

✺ This book is printed on recycled, acid-free paper containing 10% postconsumer waste.

1 2 3 4 5 6 7 8 9 0 QPD/QPD 0 9 8 7 6 5 4 3

ISBN: 0-07-282303-8

Editorial director: Tina B. Carver
Senior managing editor: Erik Gundersen
Developmental editor: Mari Vargo
Director of North American marketing: Thomas P. Dare
Director of international marketing and sales: Kate Oakes
Production manager: Genevieve Kelley

Cover designer: Mary Jane Broadbent
Interior designer: Don Kye, Think Design LLC
Copyeditor: Sophia Wisener
Skills indexer: Talbot Hamlin
Photo researcher: Kristin Thalheimer

INTERNATIONAL EDITION ISBN: 0-07-121881-5

McGraw-Hill
Contemporary

www.mhcontemporary.com

The **McGraw·Hill** Companies

ACKNOWLEDGMENTS

The author and publisher would like to thank the following individuals who reviewed the **Read On** program at various stages of development and whose comments, reviews, and assistance were instrumental in helping us shape the project:

Tony Albert
Jewish Vocational Services
San Francisco, CA

Victoria Badalamenti
LaGuardia Community College
Long Island City, NY

Lynne Telson Barsky
Suffolk Community College
Jericho, NY

Leslie Biaggi
Pembroke Pines, FL

Greg Cossu
Kyoto, Japan

Nicholas J. Dimmitt
Center for Language & Educational Technology
Asian Institute of Technology
Pathumthani, Thailand

Edna Diolata
ELESAIR Adult ESL Program
New York, NY

Deborah Horowitz
Queens College
Flushing, NY

Bea Jensen
ELESAIR Adult ESL Program
New York, NY

Tay Lesley
Culver City Adult School
Culver City, CA

Susannah O. Mackay
Atlanta, GA

Claude Mathis
El Paso Community College
El Paso, TX

Linda O'Roke
City College of San Francisco
San Francisco, CA

Jenny Outlaw
Richmond Community College
Hamlet, NC

Mary Pierce
Xavier Adult Education Center
New York, NY

Anita Podrid
Queens College
Flushing, NY

Linda Reichman
City College of San Francisco
San Francisco, CA

Jane Selden
LaGuardia Community College
Long Island City, NY

David Thormann
City College of San Francisco
San Francisco, CA

Marjorie Vai
The New School for Social Research
New York, NY

Itsuki Yasuyoshi
Waseda University
Tokyo, Japan

   I was very fortunate to receive helpful suggestions, encouragement, and advice from many people. I am especially grateful to Erik Gundersen, Acquisitions Editor, for his clear vision on this project. He is not only my editor, but also my friend. I am sincerely indebted to Mari Vargo, the developmental editor on this project. She made herself available to me around the clock, including weekends, holidays, and whenever else I needed her, and was always right on target with the endless edits involved. I am thankful to my friends at the English Language Institute at Queens College who continue to show interest and support. Last but not least, I am ever grateful to my family for allowing me the time I needed to complete this book and for helping me keep things in perspective.

–Nancy Nici Mare

TABLE OF CONTENTS

WELCOME TO READ ON 1

Chapter-opening photographs introduce students to the themes of the readings.

Before You Read activities ask students to make inferences, activate their prior knowledge, and answer questions based on their own experience.

Comprehension will increase for many students as they listen to **audio recordings** (available on cassette and CD) of the reading selections.

Selected **key vocabulary items** appear in bold-faced type in the readings.

Main Idea questions check students' understanding of what the reading selections are about.

By working with **standardized testing formats,** students prepare for success on a variety of standardized exams.

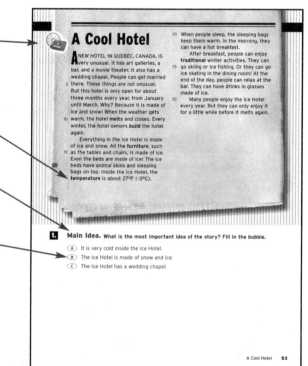

A variety of reading comprehension activities checks students' understanding of the reading passages while providing additional vocabulary practice.

Learn New Words and **Complete the Paragraph** activities test students' understanding of new vocabulary items.

In **Think It Over** activities, students use critical thinking skills to examine ideas introduced in the reading selections.

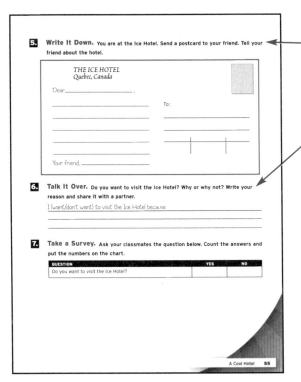

2. **Just the Facts.** Underline the correct answers. Write them on the lines.

1. The Ice Hotel is open _for three months_ . — for three months / all year
2. The Ice Hotel melts in _____. — January / March
3. People can go _____ in the dining room. — ice skating / skiing
4. The owners build the hotel again in the _____. — summer / winter
5. The temperature inside the hotel is about _____. — 27°F / -3°F

3. **Learn New Words.** Choose the correct words. Write them on the lines.

build   furniture   ~~made of~~   melts   temperature   traditional

1. This hotel is _made of_ ice and snow.
2. The _____ inside the hotel is very cold. It is only about 27°F.
3. People can go skiing or ice skating. They enjoy these _____ winter activities.
4. The hotel _____ when the weather gets warm because it is made of ice.
5. The owners _____ the hotel again every winter when the weather is cold.
6. All the _____, such as the tables and chairs, is made of ice.

4. **Think It Over.** With a partner, choose five sentences to complete the chart below.

It has art galleries.	It's made of ice and snow.
~~It is only open for three months.~~	It has a movie theater.
It has a bar.	It melts in March.
The beds are made of ice.	People can ice skate in the dining room.
It has a wedding chapel.	People can go skiing.

THE ICE HOTEL IS UNUSUAL BECAUSE...
1. It is only open for three months.
2.
3.
4.
5.

5. **Write It Down.** You are at the Ice Hotel. Send a postcard to your friend. Tell your friend about the hotel.

THE ICE HOTEL
Quebec, Canada

Dear _____ ,
_____
_____   To: _____
_____
_____
_____

Your friend, _____

6. **Talk It Over.** Do you want to visit the Ice Hotel? Why or why not? Write your reason and share it with a partner.

I (want/don't want) to visit the Ice Hotel because _____
_____
_____

7. **Take a Survey.** Ask your classmates the question below. Count the answers and put the numbers on the chart.

QUESTION	YES	NO
Do you want to visit the Ice Hotel?		

Write It Down activities ask students to write sentences and paragraphs about their thoughts, opinions, and ideas.

Talk It Over activities ask students to discuss ideas related to the chapter topics.

WELCOME TO READ ON 1

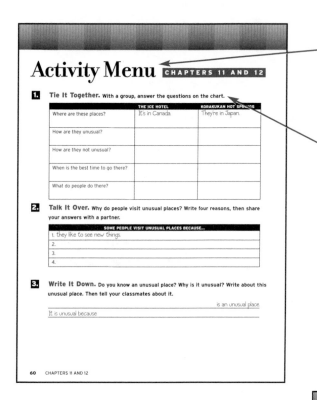

Each pair of chapters is connected by a similar theme. The **Activity Menu** ties the two chapters together, giving students opportunities to practice new vocabulary and do expansion work.

Tie It Together activities use graphic organizers to help students synthesize information from the previous two chapters.

Just for Fun activities reinforce vocabulary and give students opportunities to practice spelling and word order.

Go Online activities allow students to perform basic Internet searches.

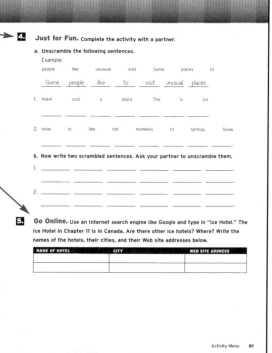

TO THE TEACHER

Read On 1 is the first in a series of two readers for beginning and high beginning students of English as a second or foreign language. **Read On 2** targets the needs of high beginning students.

Each book in the **Read On** series contains 20 four-page chapters featuring short, stimulating, and accessible reading passages on high-interest topics such as a woman who lived in a tree, a hotel made of ice, and laughter clubs that are good for your health. In addition, each reading contains vital, high frequency vocabulary that is recycled throughout the chapters in the book. This gives students a chance to see new vocabulary a number of times and in a variety of contexts.

The chapters in **Read On** are self-standing and may be used in any order. Thus, the teacher has the option of either working systematically through the book, or selecting chapters according to the needs and interests of the class.

The inclusion of a two-page Activity Menu after each pair of chapters is a unique and dynamic feature of the **Read On** series. Each Activity Menu ties together content and learning objectives from the readings in the two previous chapters, giving students additional opportunities to recycle vocabulary and do expansion work. Graphic organizers help students synthesize information from each pair of chapters and Go Online activities allow students to practice Internet search skills.

Components

The complete **Read On 1** program includes the following components:

- Student Book
- Teacher's Manual with answer key, chapter quizzes, and vocabulary cloze activities for each chapter
- Audiocassette/audio CD with recordings of all reading passages

CHAPTER 1

Twins: Will You Marry Us?

Diane and Craig

Mark and Darlene

Before You Read. Look at the pictures and read the title of the story.

1. Circle your answers and write them on the lines.

Darlene and Diane are twin ____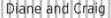____. brothers (sisters)

Mark and Craig are twin _____. brothers sisters

Craig wants to marry _____. Diane Darlene

Mark wants to marry _____. Diane Darlene

2. Answer the questions. Check (✓) Yes or No.

QUESTIONS	YES	NO
Do you know twins?		
Do they look the same?		

Twins: Will You Marry Us?

DIANE AND DARLENE NETTEMEIER are sisters. They are **identical** twins. They look the same. Diane and Darlene lived together in Missouri, in the U.S.
5 They **also** worked together. Last month, they got married together, too!

Last year, Diane and Darlene went to a twins meeting in Ohio. Many twins went there to meet other twins. Twins
10 were there from all over the U.S. The sisters met Mark and Craig Sanders there. Mark and Craig are brothers. They are also identical twins. The brothers and the sisters became good
15 friends. In fact, Mark fell in love with Darlene, and Craig fell in love with Diane. But they lived in different states. Mark and Craig lived in Texas. The brothers called the sisters **often**. They
20 sent them e-mail often, too. But they all **missed** each other a lot.

Mark and Craig had an Internet Web site. One day, they asked Darlene and Diane to go to the Web site. It said,
25 "Diane, will you marry me? Love, Craig," and "Darlene, will you marry me? Love, Mark." **Both** sisters said, "Yes!"

Today, the two couples are married.
30 They live in Texas. Diane and Darlene do not live together, but their houses are **next door** to each other. Their houses are identical, too!

1. Main Idea. What is the most important idea of the story? Fill in the bubble.

(A) Twin brothers met twin sisters at a meeting in Ohio.

(B) Two couples live next door to each other.

(C) Twin brothers married twin sisters.

2. Just the Facts. Circle the correct words. Write them on the lines.

1. Craig and Mark met Diane and Darlene in _____Ohio_____.

    Texas (Ohio)

2. The brothers married the sisters _____.

    last month   on the computer

3. Before they got married, the sisters lived in _____.

    Ohio   Missouri

4. The brothers asked the sisters to marry them _____.

    on the computer   in Ohio

5. Now the couples live in _____.

    Missouri   Texas

3. Learn New Words. Circle the correct words. Write them on the lines.

1. Diane and Darlene look _____identical_____. Mark and Craig look the same, too.

    (identical) different

2. The sisters lived together. They _____ worked together.

    also   all

3. Craig and Mark called Diane and Darlene _____. They sent a lot of e-mail, too.

    last month   often

4. They don't live together, but their houses are _____ to each other.

    different   next door

5. The brothers called the sisters and sent e-mail. The brothers _____ the sisters.

    missed   met

6. Diane and Darlene wanted to marry Craig and Mark. _____ sisters said, "Yes!"

    Some   Both

4. What Happened First? Number the sentences from 1 to 5.

_____ Diane and Craig and Darlene and Mark got married last month.

_____ They all became friends.

___1___ Twin brothers met twin sisters at a twins meeting in Ohio.

_____ The brothers called and e-mailed the sisters often.

_____ They all live in Texas now.

5. Write It Down. Write the sentences in Activity 4 in the correct order as a paragraph.

Twin brothers met twin sisters at a twins meeting in Ohio.

_____

_____

_____

_____

_____

_____

_____

6. Talk It Over. Where are some places couples meet? Write your answers below. Then share your answers with your classmates.

WHERE ARE SOME PLACES COUPLES MEET?	
1. school	5.
2. work	6.
3.	7.
4.	8.

CHAPTER 2

An Unusual Proposal

Before You Read. Look at the picture and read the title of the story.

1. The students are spelling a question. Write the question on the line.

    _____

2. Circle your answers and write them on the lines.

    The students are _____.   in the school gym   in bed

    I think _____ will get married.   a student   a teacher

3. **Answer the question. Circle Yes or No.**

    Do you help your friends?   Yes   No

An Unusual Proposal

BRIAN BATEMAN AND STACIE Martin were **neighbors**. They lived next door to each other in South Carolina, in the U.S. They
5 went to school together. They were best friends, too. But after high school, Brian and Stacie went to different colleges. Brian went to college in West Virginia. Stacie went
10 to college in Kentucky. They did not see each other often. They missed each other a lot.

Brian and Stacie finished college last year. They both returned to
15 South Carolina. Brian got a job at a hotel, and Stacie got a job at an elementary school. They became friends again. They saw each other very often. In fact, they became very
20 good friends. They fell in love.

Brian wanted to ask Stacie to marry him. He wanted to **propose** in an **unusual** way. Brian asked Stacie's students to help. He also asked
25 teachers at Stacie's school to help. The children were happy to help. They lay on the floor of the school **gym**. Their bodies **spelled** the words, "Will you marry me?" Stacie came to the
30 gym and she saw the students on the floor. She was very **confused**. The teachers asked her to stand on a ladder. She stood on the ladder and she saw the question. Then Brian
35 walked into the gym. He gave Stacie a rose. Stacie was very happy. She said, "Yes!" The students and teachers were happy about the unusual proposal, too.

---

1. **Main Idea.** What is the most important idea of the story? Fill in the bubble.

(A) Brian and Stacie wanted to get married.

(B) Brian proposed to Stacie in an unusual way.

(C) The students helped Brian propose.

2. Just the Facts. Circle **Yes** or **No**.

1. Brian and Stacie lived next door to each other.	(Yes)	No
2. Brian and Stacie went to high school together.	Yes	No
3. Brian and Stacie went to college together.	Yes	No
4. Brian and Stacie worked together.	Yes	No
5. Brian wanted to marry Stacie.	Yes	No
6. The teachers spelled the words, "Will you marry me?"	Yes	No

3. Learn New Words. Choose the correct words. Write them on the lines.

confused   fell in love   gym   ~~neighbors~~   propose   spelled   unusual

1. Brian and Stacie were ___neighbors___. They lived next door to each other.
2. Brian and Stacie became good friends. They _____ after college.
3. Brian wanted to _____ to Stacie. He wanted to marry her.
4. Stacie's students helped him in an _____ or different way.
5. They _____ "Will you marry me?" with their bodies on the gym floor.
6. Stacie was _____ when she saw her students. She didn't know why they were on the floor.
7. Then Brian walked into the _____. He gave Stacie a rose.

4. Write It Down. Write the sentences from Activity 3 as a paragraph.

Brian and Stacie were neighbors. They lived next door to each other.

_____

_____

_____

_____

_____

_____

_____

_____

5. Find the Answers. Read the questions. Find the answers in the story.

1. Where does Stacie work?

   Stacie works at ____an elementary school____.

2. Where does Brian work?

   Brian works at _____.

3. What did Brian ask the students?

   Brian asked the students _____.

4. Where did Brian propose to Stacie?

   Brian proposed to Stacie in _____.

6. Talk It Over. What things do you need help with? Who do you ask? Complete the chart with your ideas. Then share your answers with your classmates.

WHAT THINGS DO YOU NEED HELP WITH?	WHO DO YOU ASK?
my homework	my teacher or classmates

Activity Menu

1. **Tie It Together.** Look at the words below. Which words go with Chapter 1? Chapter 2? Both? With a partner, write them in the diagram below.

~~brothers~~   ~~friends~~   marry   question   teach
~~college~~   gym   neighbors   school   telephone
computer   identical   next door   sisters   twins
e-mail   ladder   proposal   students   unusual

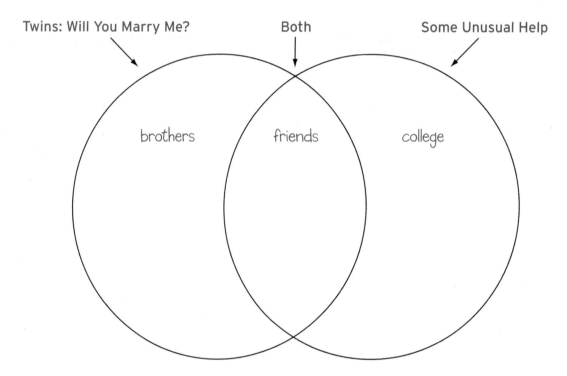

Twins: Will You Marry Me?   Both   Some Unusual Help

brothers   friends   college

2. **Write It Down.** Which proposal was more unusual, Mark and Craig's or Brian's? Circle your answer and write it on the line. Then write your reason on the next line. Share your answer with a partner.

1. _____ proposal was more unusual.

   Mark and Craig's   Brian's

2. I think it was more unusual because _____

_____

3. **Take a Survey.** How many students think Mark and Craig's proposal was more unusual? What about Brian's proposal? Put the number of students in the chart.

STATEMENTS	NUMBER OF STUDENTS
Mark and Craig's proposal was more unusual.	
Brian's proposal was more unusual.	

4. **Just for Fun.** First, complete the sentences with the correct states. Then circle the six states in the puzzle.

1. Diane and Darlene met Mark and Craig in _____Ohio_____.
2. The Nettemeier sisters lived in _____.
3. The Sanders brothers lived in _____.
4. Brian and Stacie lived next door to each other in _____.
5. Brian went to college in _____.
6. Stacie went to college in _____.

M	I	S	S	O	U	R	I	E	O	P	A	W	Y	U
T	U	K	B	J	S	H	J	S	H	I	A	W	K	N
H	H	Z	U	Q	T	D	S	B	I	G	Q	Q	C	M
U	W	O	X	F	X	V	K	Z	O	Y	X	Q	U	C
A	I	N	I	G	R	I	V	T	S	E	W	O	T	Q
S	O	U	T	H	C	A	R	O	L	I	N	A	N	F
K	O	M	R	E	F	Z	J	M	W	B	I	J	E	Y
T	W	A	J	T	X	G	R	A	Z	E	M	N	K	F
N	N	E	B	U	R	A	H	F	D	H	P	X	I	H
F	N	K	N	L	Q	Z	S	F	D	F	N	C	G	Z

5. **Go Online.** Use an Internet search engine like Google and type in "famous twins." Find the names of two pairs of famous twins. Why are they famous? Share this information with your classmates.

CHAPTER 3

What's So Funny?

Before You Read. Look at the picture and read the title of the story.

1. **Circle your answers and write them on the lines.**

These women are _____.

I _____ laugh.

I _____ every day.

laughing crying

like to don't like to

laugh don't laugh

2. **Write your answer on the line.**

Why do you think the women are laughing? _____

_____

3. **Try this. Laugh for ten seconds. How do you feel? Write your answer on the line.**

I feel _____.

What's So Funny?

IN INDIA, SOME PEOPLE MEET EVERY day in laughter clubs. For 15 or 20 minutes in the morning, they all laugh together. Sometimes they laugh **loudly**.
5 Sometimes they laugh **quietly**. No one tells jokes. No one talks. They just laugh. So, why do these people laugh?

They **laugh** because it makes them feel good. Dr. Madan Kataria agrees. He
10 started the first laughter club in Mumbai, India, in 1995. He believes that laughter is healthy. Many doctors agree with Dr. Kataria. When we laugh, we **relax**. We don't feel a lot of **stress**. This
15 can be good for our health.

At Dr. Kataria's laughter club, people do laughter exercises. First, they take several deep breaths. They breathe very slowly. Then they say "Ho-
20 Ho, Ha-Ha" together. They say it faster and faster. Then, they start to laugh. There are many other kinds of laughter exercises, too. In the "**silent** laughter" exercise, people don't make any noise.
25 In the "big laughter" exercise, everyone is very loud. In the "dancing laughter" exercise, everyone laughs and jumps at the same time.

Today, there are laughter clubs in
30 several countries in the world. More people are learning about the importance of laughter, and more people are laughing, too.

---

1.   **Main Idea.** What is the most important idea of the story? Fill in the bubble.

- (A) Laughter can be good for your health.
- (B) There are different kinds of laughter.
- (C) There is a laughter club in Mumbai.

2. Just the Facts. Circle Yes or No.

1.	People tell jokes at laughter clubs.	Yes	(No)
2.	Dr. Kataria started the first laughter club.	Yes	No
3.	There are different kinds of laughter exercises.	Yes	No
4.	When we laugh, we feel a lot of stress.	Yes	No
5.	Laughter can be good for our health.	Yes	No
6.	Laughter clubs are only in India.	Yes	No

3. Learn New Words. Circle the words that have the **opposite** meanings of the underlined words. Write them on the lines.

1. Sometimes people laugh <u>loudly</u>. But sometimes they laugh _____quietly_____.

   (quietly)   slowly

2. When we laugh, we <u>relax</u>. We don't _____.

   feel stress   feel better

3. People in the laughter clubs take deep breaths very <u>slowly</u>. Then they say
   "Ho-ho, ha-ha" _____.

   fast   quietly

4. People are <u>silent</u> in some laughter exercises, but _____ in other exercises.

   loud   happy

4. Finish the Sentences. With a partner, draw lines from the words on the left to the words on the right to complete the sentences. Then write the sentences below.

1. Everyone laughs and jumps   **a.** before the laughter exercises.
2. Everyone takes deep breaths   **b.** in the silent laughter exercise.
3. There is no noise   **c.** in the big laughter exercise.
4. Everyone is very loud   **d.** in the dancing laughter exercise.

1. <u>Everyone laughs and jumps in the dancing laughter exercise.</u>
2. _____
3. _____
4. _____ .

5. **Talk It Over.** Do you want to join a laughter club? Why or why not? Write your answer. Then share your answer with your classmates.

I (want/don't want) to join a laughter club because _____

_____

6. **Write It Down.** Look at the story again. Write five sentences about laughter clubs.

LAUGHTER CLUBS
1. Doctor Kataria started the first laughter club in 1995.
2.
3.
4.
5.

7. **Take a Survey.** What makes you laugh? Ask your classmates. Write their answers in the chart.

NAME	WHAT MAKES YOU LAUGH? (EXAMPLES: JOKES, TV SHOWS)
Erik	funny movies, jokes, silly people

CHAPTER 4

Friendship Is Good for Your Health

Before You Read. Look at the picture and read the title of the story.

1. Circle your answers and write them on the lines.

These women are _____.   happy   sad

They are _____.   at home   at a café

The women are _____.   family   friends

This story will say that friends help you feel _____.   good   bad

2. Think about your friends. What do you do together? Write three sentences.

My friends and I _____

We _____

We _____

Friendship Is Good for Your Health

GAIL CASEY WAS VERY UNHAPPY all the time. She didn't have any friends to talk to. She was **depressed**. Depression is very serious. Many
5 depressed people need **medicine** to be healthy and feel better. But some depressed people don't need medicine. They need a good friend.

Some **scientists** studied a group
10 of depressed people. They wanted to help them. They studied Gail and some other people. The scientists did not give medicine to Gail and the others. Instead, each depressed
15 person **made** a new friend. The scientists thought that friendship would make these people healthy.

Gail and her new friend, Amy, met often. They went for coffee, to dinner,
20 or to the movies together. Gail slowly started to feel better. She and Amy talked about their problems together, too. Gail had a problem with her job. She was very depressed at work. She
25 worked a lot of hours, but her boss did not give her more money. She was afraid to talk to her boss about it. Gail talked about this problem with Amy. After she talked with Amy, she
30 didn't feel afraid anymore. Then, she talked to her boss, and he **agreed** to give her more money. Now Gail is happy at work, too.

After one year, many of the other
35 people felt happy, too. They did not need medicine to feel better. Their new friends were good for their health!

---

1. **Main Idea.** What is the most important idea of the story? Fill in the bubble.

- (A) All depressed people need medicine.
- (B) Our friends can make us happy and healthy.
- (C) Gail Casey made a new friend.

2. **Just the Facts.** Underline the correct answers. Write them on the lines.

1. Friends are good for our _____health_____.   jobs   <u>health</u>

2. Gail Casey was very _____.   happy   unhappy

3. Some depressed people need _____ to   medicine   money
   feel better and be healthy.

4. Gail _____ to her boss.   talked   did not talk

5. Gail's boss _____ to give her more money.   agreed   did not agree

6. After one year, _____ of the people   all   a lot
   in the scientists' study did not need medicine.

3. **Learn New Words.** Choose the correct words. Write them on the lines.

~~depressed~~   healthy   made   medicine   scientists

1. Some scientists studied a group of _____depressed_____ people. The people were very
   unhappy.

2. A group of _____ wanted to help the people.

3. The scientists did not give _____ to the people.

4. Instead, each depressed person _____ a new friend.

5. The scientists thought that friendship would make these people _____.

4. **Finish the Sentences.** Draw lines from the words on the left to the words on the
right to complete the sentences. Then write the sentences below.

1. Amy helped   **a.** to be happy.
2. Gail's boss   **b.** made a new friend.
3. Scientists studied   **c.** some depressed people.
4. Each depressed person   **d.** Gail at work.
5. Some people did not need drugs **e.** gave Gail more money.

1. _Amy helped Gail at work._ _____

2. _____

3. _____

4. _____

5. _____

5. Find the Answers. Read the questions. Find the answers in the story.

1. Why did the scientists study depressed people?

They wanted _____

2. Why was Gail unhappy at work?

She worked a lot of hours, but _____

6. Write It Down. Look at the story again. Write two to three sentences about Gail and Amy.

Gail and Amy went for coffee. _____

_____

_____

_____

7. Talk It Over. Check (✓) the things you like to do. Add two ideas. Then share your chart with a partner.

WHAT DO YOU LIKE TO DO WITH YOUR FRIENDS?	
cook dinner	
eat at restaurants	
go to the movies	
study after class	
watch TV	
talk about problems	

Activity Menu

1. **Tie It Together.** Write each word in the correct point on the star below. Then add more words from Chapters 3 and 4. Share your work with a partner.

boss	depressed	health	jump	medicine
countries	happy	India	laugh	~~women~~

More words:

_____ _____ _____ _____

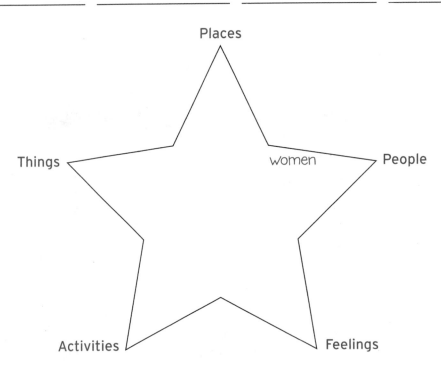

Places

Things

women

People

Activities

Feelings

2. **Write It Down.** What makes you healthy? Make a list with a group. Compare your list with another group's list.

WHAT MAKES YOU HEALTHY?	
friends	

3. **Talk It Over.** Look at the list from Activity 2. Which thing do you think is the most important? Share your ideas with a group.

I think _____ is/are most important because _____

_____

4. **Just for Fun.** With a partner, use the clues in the box to complete the puzzle.

Clues

Across

3. I have the same feeling or idea as you. We _____.

5. ~~A person who gives medicine is a _____.~~

6. We laugh at funny _____.

7. Don't talk so fast. Talk _____.

8. Not quiet

Down

1. ~~Be _____. Don't make noise.~~

2. Very unhappy

3. Gail doesn't feel unhappy _____.

4. The person you work for is your _____.

6. Your work is your _____.

CHAPTER 5

Sleeping on the Job

Before You Read. Look at the picture and read the title of the story.

1. **Circle your answers and write them on the lines.**

   This man is at _____.   home   work

   This man is _____.   sleeping   working

2. **Answer the questions. Circle your answers.**

QUESTIONS	ANSWERS	
Is it a good idea to sleep at work?	Yes	No
Do you get sleepy in the afternoon?	Yes	No

3. **Answer the question.**

   What do you do when you are sleepy in the afternoon? _____

   _____

Sleeping on the Job

MARK TASKO IS A **BUSY** MAN. HE gets up very early in the morning. He goes to bed very late at night. He works **hard** at his job every day. In the
5 afternoon, he feels tired. Some people drink coffee when they feel sleepy at work. Then they feel more **awake**. Mark does not drink coffee when he is sleepy at work. He does something different.
10 He sleeps.

Is Mark's boss angry? No. Some American companies now believe that **naps** help their workers. When people are tired, they do not do good work.
15 After they take a nap, they can do better work. In some countries, **such as** Japan, sleeping at work is not unusual. But this is a new idea in the U.S.

Some American companies now
20 have quiet nap rooms for their workers. The nap rooms have comfortable chairs and blankets. Some nap rooms have music, too. The workers can go into a nap room and sleep for **a little while**.
25 Then they go back to work.

Mark Tasko takes naps for only 15 or 20 minutes. Then he can work again. That's good for Mark Tasko, and it's good for the company, too!

1. **Main Idea.** What is the most important idea of the story? Fill in the bubble.

- (A) Workers usually nap for 15 or 20 minutes in quiet nap rooms.
- (B) Some American companies think naps help people do better work.
- (C) Quiet rooms have blankets and music so workers can relax.

2. **Just the Facts.** Check (✓) True or False. If a sentence is false, change it to make it true.

	True	False
1. People feel tired after a nap.	☐	✔

People don't feel tired after a nap.

	True	False
2. Some companies have quiet rooms for their workers.	☐	☐
3. Workers sleep at work for a long time.	☐	☐
4. Some people drink coffee when they are tired.	☐	☐
5. People do good work when they are tired.	☐	☐

3. **Learn New Words.** Circle the words that have the same meaning as the underlined words.

1. The man works hard at his job every day.
home (work)

2. People feel more awake when they drink coffee.
don't feel sleepy   are busy

3. Some people take naps at work.
sleep for a short time   sleep for a long time

4. The workers sleep for a little while.
a long time   a short time

5. In some countries, such as Japan, taking naps at work is not unusual.
also   for example

4. **Complete the Paragraph.** Use the words below to complete the paragraph.

in the morning   in the afternoon   at night   ~~busy~~   hard

Many people are very (1) _____busy_____. They work (2) _____ at their jobs every day. They go to bed very late (3) _____. They get up very early (4) _____. Sometimes they feel very tired at work (5) _____.

5. **Finish the Sentences.** With a partner, draw lines from the words on the left to the words on the right to complete the sentences. Then write the sentences below.

1. Some workers take naps because
2. Workers can nap in
3. They sleep for
4. Some people drink coffee
5. Some American companies believe that

a. naps help the workers.
b. to feel more awake.
c. they are tired.
d. 15 or 20 minutes.
e. a quiet room.

1. Some workers take naps because they are tired.
2. _____
3. _____
4. _____
5. _____

6. **Write It Down.** Write three sentences about Mark Tasko.

In the morning, Mark Tasko _____
In the afternoon, _____
At night, _____

7. **Talk It Over.** Answer the questions. Circle your choices and complete the sentences. Share your answers with a partner.

1. You are a boss. Can your workers take naps at work?
   The workers (can/can not) take naps at work because _____

   _____

2. You are a worker. Do you want to take naps at work?
   I (want/do not want) to take naps at work because _____

   _____

CHAPTER 6

The Home Office

Before You Read. Look at the picture and read the title of the story.

1. **Answer the questions. Check (✓) Yes, No, or I don't know.**

QUESTIONS	YES	NO	I DON'T KNOW
Is this person at home?			
Is this person at work?			
Does this person have a job?			
Do you have a job?			
Can you work at home?			

2. **Write your answer on the line. Share your answer with your classmates.**

Some people work at home. Why do you think they work at home? Write one reason:

_____

The Home Office

KATE SIMON GETS UP IN THE morning. She eats breakfast. She showers. She gets dressed for work. But she does not leave her house.
5 Kate works at home. These days, many people work at home. They are called "telecommuters."

Telecommuters don't **commute**, or drive, to their jobs. They use
10 computers, telephones, and fax machines to "talk" to their **coworkers**. Every year, more companies let employees work at home. Some workers, like Kate, enjoy
15 working at home.

"I can choose my hours. I can wear comfortable clothes. And I don't have to drive or take a **crowded** bus every day. It's cheaper, too. I don't
20 pay for a bus ride, or buy gas for my car," says Kate.

Many telecommuters agree with Kate. But David Park does not agree. David was a telecommuter for two
25 years. He missed his coworkers. He had no one to talk to. He had no one to **discuss** his ideas with. Also, David thinks that telecommuters work more hours. "When you work in an office,
30 your work is **finished** when you go home. When you work at home, your work is never finished," says David. "In fact, I often worked on weekends and on vacations, too."
35 Telecommuting is not good for everyone. David Park does not work at home anymore. But for some people, like Kate Simon, it's the best choice.

---

1. **Main Idea.** What is the most important idea of the story? Fill in the bubble.

- (A) Kate Simon works at home.
- (B) Some people telecommute, or work at home.
- (C) Telecommuters work on weekends.

2. Just the Facts. Underline the correct answers. Write them on the lines.

1. _____ Kate _____ likes to work at home. David   <u>Kate</u>

2. David Park _____ his coworkers.   missed   talked to

3. Telecommuters _____ their jobs.   drive to   don't drive to

4. David _____ at home anymore.   works   doesn't work

5. Telecommuters can choose their _____ .   hours   jobs

3. Learn New Words. Circle the words that have the same meaning as the underlined words.

1. Telecommuters don't <u>commute to their jobs</u> because they work at home.
   use a computer at work   (go to their offices)

2. Kate doesn't take <u>a crowded bus</u> every day because she works at home.
   a quiet bus   a bus full of people

3. Telecommuters can <u>choose their hours</u>: morning, afternoon, or night.
   decide when to work   enjoy their work

4. David wanted to <u>discuss</u> his ideas with other people. He missed his coworkers.
   think about   talk about

5. When you work at home, your work is never <u>finished</u>. Sometimes you work on weekends.
   done   good

4. Complete the Paragraph. Use the words below to complete the paragraph.

agree   coworkers   employees   ~~enjoys~~   pay for

Kate likes her job. She (1) ____enjoys____ working at home. She doesn't have to
(2) _____ a bus ride. Many workers (3) _____ with Kate. They like to
work at home, too. But some (4) _____ do not. David worked at home. He did not
talk to his (5) _____ because he worked alone.

5. **Think It Over.** With a partner, circle the correct words. Write each sentence on the correct side of the chart.

~~He/She can choose his/her hours.~~ (He/She and his/her circled)

He/She doesn't have to drive.

He/She missed his/her coworkers.

It's cheaper for him/her.

His/Her work was never finished.

He/She worked on weekends.

KATE SIMON LIKES TO WORK AT HOME BECAUSE...	DAVID PARK DOESN'T LIKE TO WORK AT HOME BECAUSE...
She can choose her hours.	

6. **Write It Down.** Look at the story again. Write a paragraph about David Park.

David Park works in an office now. He likes it because _____

_____

_____

_____

7. **Talk It Over.** Do you want to work at home? Talk with a partner. Then complete the sentence below.

I (want/don't want) to work at home because _____

_____

_____

_____

8. **Take a Survey.** Ask your classmates this question. Count their answers and put the numbers on the chart.

QUESTION	YES	NO
Do you want to work at home?		

Activity Menu

1. **Tie It Together.** Look at the words below. Which words go with Chapter 5? Chapter 6? Both? With a partner, write them in the diagram below.

~~awake~~	computer	Japan	sleepy	vacation
boss	coworkers	job	~~telecommuter~~	weekend
busy	employee	nap	telephone	~~work~~
company	home	office	tired	workers

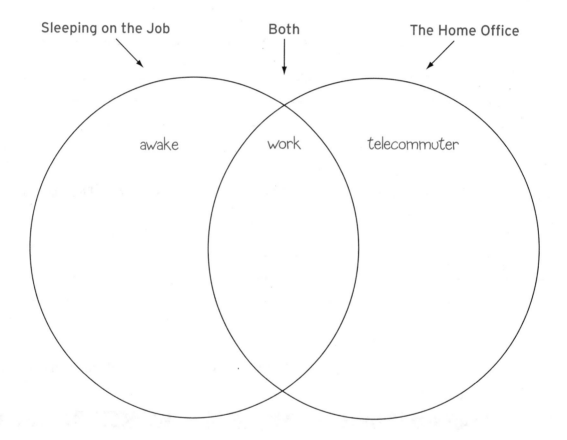

Sleeping on the Job   Both   The Home Office

awake   work   telecommuter

2. **Take a Survey.** Ask your classmates the questions below. Count their answers and write the numbers in the chart.

QUESTIONS	YES	NO
Do you want to take naps at work?		

3. **Find the Answers.** Read the questions. With a partner, find the answers in the stories. Check (✓) the correct answer.

QUESTIONS	MARK TASKO	KATE SIMON	DAVID PARK
Who likes to work at home?		✓	
Who takes a nap at work?			
Who worked on the weekends?			
Who wears comfortable clothes at work?			
Who is sometimes tired at work?			
Who missed his coworkers?			

4. **Talk It Over.** People like their jobs for many reasons. Write five reasons on the chart below. Share your reasons with a group.

SOME PEOPLE LIKE THEIR JOBS BECAUSE...	
they can take naps at work.	

5. **Just for Fun.** Unscramble each word. Then use the numbered letters to make a word in the boxes below.

SISUSCD D □ □ □ □ □
                 3 6

GAREE A □ □ □
           2

WEAKA A □ □ □
            7

RYAMEON A □ □ □ □ □
        5 4 8 1

T L □ □ □ □ M T □
1   2   3 4 5   6   7 8

CHAPTER 7

No Homework Tonight

Before You Read. Look at the picture and read the title of the story.

1. Circle your answers and write them on the lines.

   _____ give homework.   Students   Teachers

   Students do homework at _____.   school   home

2. Answer the questions. Circle **Yes** or **No.** Share your answers with your classmates.

QUESTIONS	ANSWERS	
Do all teachers give homework?	Yes	No
Do most children like homework?	Yes	No
Do you like homework?	Yes	No
Did you have a lot of homework as a child?	Yes	No

No Homework Tonight

KYOKO OSAKI WORKS HARD IN school all day. But when she comes home, she has more work: homework. Kyoko does homework for two hours
5 every night. How old is Kyoko? She is only eight years old. Kyoko goes to school in Tokyo, Japan. In Japan, children often have **a lot of** homework after school. They also have homework on
10 **weekends.** That is not unusual. In fact, children have a lot of homework in many countries in the world. But in one city in the U.S., children have **almost no** homework.
15　　Michael Lee is a student in an elementary school in Piscataway, New

Jersey. He is eight years old, like Kyoko. But he only has a little bit of homework each night: about **half an hour.** He does
20 not have any homework on weekends. Why? His parents don't want him to have a lot of homework.
　　Many parents in Michael's school agree. They work hard all day at their
25 jobs. When they come home, they want to enjoy family time with their children. The parents want time to talk with their children. They want time to eat **dinner** with their children, too. But homework
30 takes a lot of time.
　　The parents talked about this homework **problem** with the teachers, and the teachers agreed. Now the students only have a little bit of
35 homework every night.

1.　**Main Idea.** What is the most important idea of the story? Fill in the bubble.

(A)　Teachers give a lot of homework in many countries in the world.

(B)　Some parents in New Jersey do not want their children to have a lot of homework.

(C)　Michael only has half an hour of homework every night.

2. Just the Facts. Which sentences are true? Circle the letters of the true sentences.

1. **(a.)** Parents in one New Jersey school did not want a lot of homework.
   b. Parents in one New Jersey school wanted a lot of homework.

2. **a.** Some students in Piscataway, New Jersey, have no homework at night.
   b. Some students in Piscataway, New Jersey, have only a little bit of homework.

3. **a.** Michael's parents wanted a lot of homework for Michael.
   b. Michael's parents wanted a little bit of homework for Michael.

4. **a.** The New Jersey teachers agreed with the parents.
   b. The New Jersey teachers did not agree with the parents.

3. Learn New Words. Circle the words that have the same meaning as the underlined words.

1. In one city in the U.S., children have almost no homework. They can enjoy time with their families after school.   (a little bit of)   a lot of

2. Many parents agreed with Michael's parents. They thought Michael's parents were right.
   had the same idea as   had a different idea than

3. Michael doesn't have any homework on weekends. He can have fun with his family.
   Monday to Friday   Saturdays and Sundays

4. Michael only has half an hour of homework every night. That isn't a lot.
   60 minutes   30 minutes

4. Think It Over. With a partner, circle the letters of the correct answers.

1. The parents talked about a problem with the teachers. The problem is:
   a. homework takes a lot of family time.
   b. Michael only has a little homework every night.

2. Parents want to eat dinner with their children after work. They eat dinner:
   a. in the morning.
   b. at night.

5. Finish the Sentences. With a partner, draw lines from the words on the left to the words on the right to complete the sentences. Then write the sentences below.

1. Kyoko has
2. Michael has
3. The teachers agreed
4. The parents want to
5. The children in the New Jersey school have no

a. enjoy time with their children.
b. homework on weekends.
c. only a little bit of homework.
d. with the parents.
e. a lot of homework.

1. Kyoko has a lot of homework.
2. _____
3. _____
4. _____
5. _____

6. Write It Down. Michael's parents want to enjoy family time. Write two examples of family time.

Example: Eating dinner together

1. _____
2. _____

7. Talk It Over. Do children need homework? Complete the chart below. Then share your answers with your classmates.

CHILDREN'S AGE	DO THEY NEED HOMEWORK? YES OR NO	HOW MUCH HOMEWORK? (HOURS/MINUTES)
7		
10		
13		
15		

CHAPTER 8

Learning Online

Before You Read. Look at the picture and read the title of the story.

1. **Circle your answers and write them on the lines.**

   This woman is _____.   doing homework   talking on the phone

   She is studying _____.   at home   in class

2. **Work with a partner. Make a list of things people can do online.**

WHAT CAN PEOPLE DO ONLINE?
1.
2.
3.

Learning Online

MAY PING IS A STUDENT AT Bellevue Community College **near** Seattle, Washington, in the U.S. But she doesn't live in
5 Washington. In fact, she doesn't live in the U.S. May lives on a small island near Australia.

May **takes** classes through the Internet. She wanted to study at an
10 American college. But she did not want to leave her home. Now she studies English and computer science **online**. May is a student in Bellevue Community College's distance
15 learning program.

May is an online student. Online students buy their books through the Internet. They do homework every week like other students. They write
20 compositions and take **exams**, too. The online students send their work to their teachers by e-mail. The teachers correct the work and return it by e-mail, too.

25 May thinks distance learning is **helpful**. Terry Hong agrees with May. Terry is a student at Bellevue Community College, too. She studies mathematics and biology. She lives
30 near the college. In fact, she can drive there in half an hour. But she studies online. Terry is a parent. She has two young children. She has almost no time to study. She has to
35 study at night and on weekends. It is not easy for her to go to class. Now she can go to college and stay at home at the same time. Some students at Bellevue Community
40 College go to the college to take classes. But others take classes online, **like** May and Terry.

---

1. **Main Idea.** **What is the most important idea of the story? Fill in the bubble.**

- (A) Students at an American college can take college classes online.
- (B) Terry Hong has two children.
- (C) Online students do homework every week.

2. Just the Facts. Circle Yes or No.

1.	May Ping lives in the U.S.	Yes	(No)
2.	May Ping takes classes at an American college.	Yes	No
3.	Terry Hong is an online student.	Yes	No
4.	Online students have no homework.	Yes	No
5.	Terry Hong lives in the U.S.	Yes	No

3. Learn New Words. Choose the correct words. Write them on the lines.

exams   helpful   ~~like~~   near   others   takes

1. Online students do homework every week _____like_____ other students.

2. Distance learning is _____ for Terry. She can stay home.

3. Some students study online, but _____ go to the college.

4. Terry lives _____ the college. She can drive there in half an hour.

5. May _____ classes through the Internet. She doesn't drive to the college.

6. Online students take _____ and write compositions. They send their tests and papers to their teachers by e-mail.

4. Finish the Sentences. With a partner, draw lines from the words on the left to the words on the right to complete the sentences. Then write the sentences below.

1. May Ping lives	**a.**	taking classes through the Internet.
2. Terry Hong lives	**b.**	books through the Internet.
3. Online students buy	**c.**	in Washington.
4. Online students send	**d.**	on an island near Australia.
5. Distance learning is	**e.**	work to teachers by e-mail.

1. May Ping lives on an island near Australia. _____

2. _____

3. _____

4. _____

5. _____

5. Think It Over. With a partner, write each sentence on the correct side of the chart.

~~She lives in the U.S.~~

She lives near Australia.

She studies English and computer science.

She is a parent.

She didn't want to leave her country.

She studies mathematics and biology.

MAY PING	TERRY HONG
	She lives in the U.S.

6. Write It Down. Do you want to study online? Why or why not? Complete the sentence.

I (want/don't want) to study online because _____

_____

7. Talk It Over. Read sentences about five college students. Can distance learning be helpful for them? Check (✓) **Yes** or **No**. Then, add two more sentences to the chart. Share your answers with a partner. Ask your partner to check (✓) Yes or No for your two sentences.

CAN DISTANCE LEARNING BE HELPFUL FOR THESE PEOPLE?	YES	NO
Mary has three young children.	✓	
Thomas works all day.		
Chris likes to meet other students.		
John does not live near a college.		
Lauren likes to talk to her teachers.		

Activity Menu

1. **Tie It Together.** Complete the chart below with a partner. Check (✓) the correct names.

QUESTIONS	KYOKO OSAKI	MICHAEL LEE	MAY PING	TERRY HONG
Who lives in the U.S.?		✓		✓
Who doesn't live in the U.S.?				
Who has children?				
Who is a child?				
Who is a student?				
Who takes classes through the Internet?				
Who has homework?				
Who sends e-mail to the teacher?				
Who lives in Japan?				

2. **Write It Down.** Use the phrases below to complete the chart.

a little bit of homework   too much homework

an American college   Internet

family time   leave her country

his teachers   online student

PROBLEM:	Michael Lee had _too much homework_. His parents wanted to enjoy _____. ↓	May Ping wanted to study in _____. She did not want to _____. ↓
SOLUTION:	Michael's parents talked to _____. Now he only has _____.	She takes classes through the _____. She is an _____.

3. **Talk It Over.** Most children do homework after school. What other things do children do after school? Make a list. Share it with your classmates.

THINGS THAT CHILDREN DO AFTER SCHOOL	
homework	

4. **Just for Fun.** Unscramble these new words. Then use the letters in the circles to make a word in the boxes below.

TECHARE   Ⓣ □ □ □ ◯

ECSANDIT   D ◯ □ ◯ □ ◯ □

WMOHOKRE   H □ ◯ □ □

NEEWEDK   W □ □ □ ◯

PLFEHLU   H ◯ □ □ □ □

□ I □ □ □ □ □ □ □

5. **Go Online.** Find Web sites for two colleges near your home. Use an Internet search engine like Google and type in "college" and your city and state, or your city and country. Write the names of the colleges and their Web site addresses below.

NAME OF COLLEGE	WEB SITE ADDRESS

CHAPTER 9

Visiting Pets

Before You Read. Look at the picture and read the title of the story.

1. **Circle your answers and write them on the lines.**

This woman is in a wheelchair because she _____.	is tired	can't walk
The young woman is her _____.	nurse	friend
The woman feels _____ because of the dog.	good	bad

2. **Ask three classmates this question. Discuss your answers together.**

NAME	DO YOU HAVE A PET? NO I DON'T, BECAUSE...	YES, I DO. I HAVE A...

Visiting Pets

KIM THOMAS HAD A VERY BAD CAR accident. She was in the **hospital**. She was depressed and lonely, and she felt terrible. Life was difficult for her.
5 Then one day Bonnie came to her room. She sat quietly on Kim's bed. She stayed with Kim when she slept, too. Kim felt better when Bonnie came to see her. Who is Bonnie? She is a dog.
10   People take good care of their **pets**. But some pets, like Bonnie, take care of people now. This is called pet therapy. The pets visit children and adults in hospitals. Some doctors believe it is
15 very helpful. At Edward Hospital near Chicago, Illinois, in the U.S., doctors think that the pets help **patients**, or sick people, feel better. The doctors **bring** animals to visit the patients. The
20 patients feel calm when the pets visit them. They smile more, too. Some pets also go to nursing homes to visit elderly people. The pets are happy to see the people. The elderly people are
25 happy to see the pets, too.

    Kim Thomas **got better** fast. She left the hospital after a few weeks. The doctors believe that Bonnie helped Kim. Kim agrees. Today, only a few doctors
30 use pet therapy. In the future, more doctors will use pets to help their patients. And they will use many different animals such as cats, dogs, and birds.

---

1.   **Main Idea.** **What is the most important idea of the story? Fill in the bubble.**

   Ⓐ   Many people have pets, such as cats and dogs.

   Ⓑ   Animals can help people feel better.

   Ⓒ   Sick children enjoy pets.

2. Just the Facts. Circle the correct answers. Write them on the lines.

1. Bonnie is a _____pet_____.
   (pet) patient

2. Kim Thomas is a _____.
   patient   doctor

3. Some doctors think people feel _____ with pets.
   better   lonely

4. Patients _____ more when they see the pets.
   eat   smile

5. People don't feel _____ when pets visit.
   happy   lonely

3. Learn New Words. Circle the words that have the same meaning as the underlined words.

1. Pets go to hospitals to visit sick people. They also go to nursing homes to visit underline{elderly} people.
   young   sick   (old)

2. Doctors believe pets help underline{patients} in hospitals feel better.
   sick people   children   senior citizens

3. Patients often feel underline{calm} when they are with pets. They don't feel stress.
   relaxed   happy   sick

4. The doctors underline{bring} animals to visit the patients at the hospitals.
   ask   help   take

4. Complete the Paragraph. Use the words below to complete the paragraph.

car accident   got better   hospital   stayed   terrible

Kim Thomas had a very bad (1) _____car accident_____. She was in the hospital.
She felt (2) _____. She was lonely and depressed. Bonnie
(3) _____ with Kim when she slept. Kim (4) _____ fast.
She left the (5) _____ after a few weeks.

5. **Finish the Sentences.** With a partner, draw lines from the words on the left to the words on the right to complete the sentences. Then write the sentences below.

1. Some pets go to nursing homes
2. Kim felt better
3. Pet therapy is when
4. Kim felt depressed
5. Kim was in the hospital because

a. before Bonnie visited her.
b. after Bonnie visited her.
c. to visit elderly people.
d. she had a car accident.
e. animals take care of people.

1. Some pets go to nursing homes to visit elderly people.
2. _____
3. _____
4. _____
5. _____

6. **Talk It Over.** What animals do you think are good for pet therapy? Make a list. Share it with a partner.

ANIMALS FOR PET THERAPY	
dogs	

7. **Write It Down.** Choose one kind of animal from Activity 6. Why is this animal good for pet therapy? Complete the sentences.

I think _____ are good for pet therapy. They are good because _____
_____

CHAPTER 10

Guide Horses

Before You Read. Look at the pictures and read the title of the story.

1. **Circle your answers and write them on the lines.**

   The man in these pictures can't _____ .   see   hear

   The horse _____ him.   helps   doesn't help

2. **Read the sentences. Check (✓) your answers on the left. After you read the story, check your answers on the right.**

BEFORE YOU READ		HORSES	AFTER YOU READ	
AGREE	DISAGREE		AGREE	DISAGREE
		All horses are very large.		
		Horses can be helpful to blind people.		
		All horses are difficult to take care of.		
		Horses live longer than dogs live.		

Guide Horses

DAN SHAW IS BLIND. WHEN HE walks down the street, people **stare** at him. They look at him because he has Cuddles. Cuddles is his guide horse. She is a **miniature** horse. In fact, Cuddles is only 26 inches high!

Sometimes, blind people have guide dogs to help them. But some blind people don't like dogs. They may be afraid of dogs. They may be **allergic** to dogs. Now, they can have guide horses instead.

Dan Shaw was the first person to have a guide horse. Cuddles helps him a lot. Guide horses are very small, but they are very **strong**. One day, Dan and Cuddles were on a busy street. Suddenly, a bicycle came towards them. Cuddles used her strong body. She pushed Dan out of the way. The horses have good memories, too. Cuddles can **remember** how to go to different places with Dan, such as the grocery store or the post office.

Miniature horses live a long time. Some miniature horses live for about 40 years. Most dogs only live for about 15 years. Guide horses do not have to live inside, like dogs do. They can live outside. But they need a home with a big **backyard**. This is because they eat a lot of grass.

Many blind people want guide horses like Cuddles. Right now, there are **only a few**. But soon, there will be more.

---

1. **Main Idea.** What is the most important idea of the story? Fill in the bubble.

(A) Guide horses can be very helpful to blind people.

(B) Some people are afraid of dogs.

(C) Cuddles can remember how to go to different places with Dan.

2. Just the Facts. Which sentences are true? Circle the letters of the true sentences.

1. **a.** All blind people have guide dogs.
   (b.) Some blind people have guide dogs.
2. **a.** Guide horses are miniature horses.
   b. Guide horses are large horses.
3. **a.** Guide horses have to live in a house.
   b. Guide dogs have to live in a house.
4. **a.** Guide horses live for 26 years.
   b. Guide horses live for 40 years.
5. **a.** Guide dogs need a home with a big backyard.
   b. Guide horses need a home with a big backyard.

3. Learn New Words. Choose the correct words. Write them on the lines.

| allergic | ~~difficult~~ | only a few | remember | stare |

1. Life is not easy for blind people. It can be very ___difficult___.
2. There are not many guide horses. In fact, there are _____.
3. People look at Dan when he walks down the street. They _____ at him because he has Cuddles.
4. Cuddles has a good memory. She can _____ how to go to many places with Dan.
5. Some people sneeze when they are near dogs. They are _____ to dogs.

4. Complete the Paragraph. Use the words below to complete the paragraph.

| backyard | ~~miniature~~ | memories | strong |

Horses like Cuddles are called (1) ___miniature___ horses because they are very small. They can remember many places because they have good (2) _____. Guide horses are useful on busy streets because they are (3) _____. They need a big (4) _____ because they eat a lot of grass.

5. Talk It Over. Read about the people on the chart. Which is better for each person: a guide dog or a guide horse? Check (✓) the correct column. Share your answers with a partner.

PERSON	GUIDE HORSE	GUIDE DOG
Anna is allergic to dogs.	✓	
Sandy lives in a big house with a big yard.		
Brian lives in a small apartment.		
Daniel is afraid of dogs.		
Andrew does not like horses.		
Jay walks to work in a busy city.		

6. Write It Down. Some blind people want guide dogs and some want guide horses. Complete the sentences below. Write two reasons for each.

Some blind people want guide dogs because _____

_____

_____

Some blind people want guide horses because _____

_____

_____

7. Take a Survey. How many students think a guide horse is better? How many students think a guide dog is better? Take a class survey. Count the answers and put the numbers in the chart.

STATEMENTS	NUMBER OF STUDENTS
A guide horse is better.	
A guide dog is better.	

Activity Menu

1. **Tie It Together.** The sentences on the chart describe pet therapy animals and guide horses. Which kind of animal does each sentence describe? Check (✓) the correct column.

DESCRIPTION	PET THERAPY ANIMALS ONLY	GUIDE HORSES ONLY	BOTH
They are calm.			✓
They can live outside.			
They are helpful.			
They visit people in the hospital.			
They are strong.			
They help patients feel better.			
They can sit quietly.			
They have good memories.			
They are small.			
They need a big backyard.			

2. **Talk It Over.** Look at the list in Activity 1. In your opinion, which description is the most important for a pet therapy animal? For a guide horse? Complete the chart below. Talk about your reasons with a partner.

ANIMALS	MOST IMPORTANT DESCRIPTION
Pet therapy animals	
Guide horses	

3. **Write It Down.** Look at Activity 2. Complete the sentences below. Write your reasons.

Pet therapy animals _____

This is important because _____

Guide horses _____

This is important because _____

4. **Just for Fun.** Find and circle the words in the puzzle.

E	B	V	L	M	L	Y	P	D	H
Y	D	A	T	J	R	U	E	Y	O
N	L	I	C	O	I	S	T	L	S
S	W	R	M	K	S	N	S	E	P
X	T	E	E	E	Y	D	C	N	I
D	M	A	R	D	K	A	T	O	T
D	R	P	R	D	L	C	R	L	A
R	E	K	A	E	G	E	G	D	L
D	S	T	N	E	I	T	A	P	B
A	L	L	E	R	G	I	C	F	L

Word List

allergic
backyard
depressed
elderly
hospital
lonely
memory
patients
pets
stare

5. **Go Online.** Find two Web sites about pet therapy. Use an Internet search engine like Google and type in "pet therapy." Write the Web site addresses below.

_____   _____

CHAPTER 11

A Cool Hotel

Before You Read. Look at the picture and read the title of the story.

1. **Circle your answers and write them on the lines.**

This hotel is made of _____.	ice	glass
It is _____.	summer	winter
This hotel is _____.	new	old

2. **Ask a partner these questions. Check (✓) Yes or No.**

QUESTIONS	YES	NO
Do you like to travel?		
Do you like hotels?		
Do you like cold weather?		
Do you like snow?		

A Cool Hotel

A NEW HOTEL IN QUEBEC, CANADA, IS very unusual. It has art galleries, a bar, and a movie theater. It also has a wedding chapel. People can get married there. These things are not unusual. But this hotel is only open for about three months every year, from January until March. Why? Because it is made of ice and snow! When the weather gets warm, the hotel **melts** and closes. Every winter, the hotel owners **build** the hotel again.

Everything in the Ice Hotel is made of ice and snow. All the **furniture**, such as the tables and chairs, is made of ice. Even the beds are made of ice! The ice beds have animal skins and sleeping bags on top. Inside the Ice Hotel, the **temperature** is about 27°F (-3°C).

When people sleep, the sleeping bags keep them warm. In the morning, they can have a hot breakfast.

After breakfast, people can enjoy **traditional** winter activities. They can go skiing or ice fishing. Or they can go ice skating in the dining room! At the end of the day, people can relax at the bar. They can have drinks in glasses made of ice.

Many people enjoy the Ice Hotel every year. But they can only enjoy it for a little while before it melts again.

---

1. **Main Idea.** What is the most important idea of the story? Fill in the bubble.

- Ⓐ It is very cold inside the Ice Hotel.
- Ⓑ The Ice Hotel is made of snow and ice.
- Ⓒ The Ice Hotel has a wedding chapel.

2. Just the Facts. Underline the correct answers. Write them on the lines.

1. The Ice Hotel is open __for three months__ .   for three months   all year

2. The Ice Hotel melts in _____ .   January   March

3. People can go _____ in the dining room.   ice skating   skiing

4. The owners build the hotel again in the _____ .   summer   winter

5. The temperature inside the hotel is about _____ .   27ºF   -3ºF

3. Learn New Words. Choose the correct words. Write them on the lines.

build   furniture   ~~made of~~   melts   temperature   traditional

1. This hotel is _____made of_____ ice and snow.

2. The _____ inside the hotel is very cold. It is only about 27ºF.

3. People can go skiing or ice skating. They enjoy these _____ winter activities.

4. The hotel _____ when the weather gets warm because it is made of ice.

5. The owners _____ the hotel again every winter when the weather is cold.

6. All the _____ , such as the tables and chairs, is made of ice.

4. Think It Over. With a partner, choose five sentences to complete the chart below.

It has art galleries.

~~It is only open for three months.~~

It has a bar.

The beds are made of ice.

It has a wedding chapel.

It's made of ice and snow.

It has a movie theater.

It melts in March.

People can ice skate in the dining room.

People can go skiing.

THE ICE HOTEL IS UNUSUAL BECAUSE...
1. It is only open for three months.
2.
3.
4.
5.

5. **Write It Down.** You are at the Ice Hotel. Send a postcard to your friend. Tell your friend about the hotel.

THE ICE HOTEL
Quebec, Canada

Dear_____,

_____

_____   To:

_____   _____

_____   _____

_____

Your friend, _____

6. **Talk It Over.** Do you want to visit the Ice Hotel? Why or why not? Write your reason and share it with a partner.

I (want/don't want) to visit the Ice Hotel because _____

_____

_____

7. **Take a Survey.** Ask your classmates the question below. Count the answers and put the numbers on the chart.

QUESTION	YES	NO
Do you want to visit the Ice Hotel?		

CHAPTER 12

A Monkey Bath

Before You Read. Look at the picture and read the title of the story.

1. **Circle your answers and write them on the lines.**

   These monkeys are in _____.   a hot spring   a bathtub

   The monkeys are _____.   relaxing   eating

2. **Answer the question on the chart. Check (✓) the choices that are true for you. Then add two ideas.**

HOW DO YOU RELAX?			
I read a book.		I listen to music.	
I take a bath.			
I take a nap.			

A Monkey Bath

THERE ARE MANY BEAUTIFUL **HOT springs** in Japan. Many people visit these warm baths. The temperature of the baths is about 122°F (50°C).
5 People relax and enjoy the warm water and the beautiful scenery. People can relax in the hot springs alone or with other people. But at the Korakukan baths in Nagano, Japan,
10 people can also relax with monkeys! These snow monkeys live in the mountains. They come to the hot springs in the morning. They enjoy the warm baths, too!
15 The snow monkeys live in Wild Monkey Park. The park is **near** the hot springs. There are about 270 snow monkeys in the park. The Japanese government **protects** them.
20 The monkeys are **gentle**, but they are not like pets. You can't touch them because they can bite or scratch you. Also, you can't feed them. But you can sit quietly and take a bath with
25 them!
    The snow monkeys sleep in the trees at night. They enjoy the warm baths in the morning. About 30 years ago, a snow monkey came to the hot
30 springs for the first time. She put her hand into the bath to get some food. The monkey enjoyed the warm water very much. She sat in the bath. Soon other snow monkeys came to the hot
35 springs, too. Now, they come every day, **especially** in the cold winter.

---

1. **Main Idea.** What is the most important idea of the story? Fill in the bubble.

(A) Snow monkeys live in Wild Monkey Park in the mountains of Nagano.

(B) People can enjoy many hot springs in Nagano, Japan.

(C) People and monkeys enjoy the hot springs at the Korakukan baths.

2. **Just the Facts.** Underline the correct answers. Write them on the lines.

1. People visit the hot springs to relax and enjoy _____ the scenery _____.

the scenery   Wild Monkey Park

2. The snow monkeys live in _____.

the hot springs   Wild Monkey Park

3. The snow monkeys sleep in the trees _____.

at night   in the morning

4. The snow monkeys enjoy the hot springs _____.

at night   in the morning

5. The temperature in the baths is about _____.

122°C   50°C

6. Snow monkeys came to the hot springs about 30 years ago for the _____.

first time   scenery

3. **Learn New Words.** Choose the correct words. Write them on the lines.

especially   gentle   ~~hot springs~~   near   protects

1. Many people visit the _____ hot springs _____ in Japan. They relax in the warm baths.

2. Wild Monkey Park is _____ the warm baths in Nagano.

3. The Japanese government _____ the monkeys there. The government wants the monkeys to be safe.

4. The monkeys come to enjoy the warm water every day, _____ in the cold winter.

5. The monkeys are _____, but they are not like pets.

4. **Talk It Over.** Complete the chart below. Share your answer with a partner.

QUESTION	YES	NO	REASON
Do you want to sit in the hot springs with a snow monkey?			

5. **Think It Over.** Check (✓) the correct columns. Share your answers with your classmates.

STATEMENTS	MONKEYS ONLY	PETS ONLY	MONKEYS AND PETS
They are gentle.			✓
You can touch them.			
You can't touch them.			
You can feed them.			
You can't feed them.			
They can bite or scratch you.			

6. **Write It Down.** Write four sentences about snow monkeys.

1. Snow monkeys enjoy _____

2. Snow monkeys live _____

3. Snow monkeys sleep _____

4. Snow monkeys are _____

7. **Take a Survey.** How many students want to sit in the hot springs with snow monkeys? How many do not? Take a class survey. Count the answers and put the numbers in the chart.

STATEMENT	NUMBER OF STUDENTS
I want to sit in the hot springs with snow monkeys.	
I don't want to sit in the hot springs with snow monkeys.	

Activity Menu

1. **Tie It Together.** With a group, answer the questions on the chart.

	THE ICE HOTEL	KORAKUKAN HOT SPRINGS
Where are these places?	It's in Canada.	They're in Japan.
How are they unusual?		
How are they not unusual?		
When is the best time to go there?		
What do people do there?		

2. **Talk It Over.** Why do people visit unusual places? Write four reasons, then share your answers with a partner.

SOME PEOPLE VISIT UNUSUAL PLACES BECAUSE...
1. they like to see new things.
2.
3.
4.

3. **Write It Down.** Do you know an unusual place? Why is it unusual? Write about this unusual place. Then tell your classmates about it.

_____ is an unusual place.

It is unusual because _____

4. Just for Fun. Complete the activity with a partner.

a. Unscramble the following sentences.

Example:

| people | like | unusual | visit | Some | places | to |

Some people like to visit unusual places.

1. Hotel   cool   a   place.   The   is   Ice

_____ _____ _____ _____ _____ _____ _____ .

2. relax   in   like   hot   monkeys   to   springs.   Snow

_____ _____ _____ _____ _____ _____ _____ _____ .

b. Now write two scrambled sentences. Ask your partner to unscramble them.

1. _____ _____ _____ _____ _____

   _____ _____ _____ _____ _____ .

2. _____ _____ _____ _____ _____

   _____ _____ _____ _____ _____ .

5. Go Online. Use an Internet search engine like Google and type in "Ice Hotel." The Ice Hotel in Chapter 11 is in Canada. Are there other ice hotels? Where? Write the names of the hotels, their cities, and their Web site addresses below.

NAME OF HOTEL	CITY	WEB SITE ADDRESS

CHAPTER 13

The Bear Man

Before You Read. Look at the picture and read the title of the story.

1. **Circle your answers and write them on the lines.**

   What kind of animal is this? _____   A grizzly bear   A lion

   Is this animal dangerous? _____   Yes   No

2. **Answer the questions. Write your answers on the left. After you read the story, write your answers on the right.**

BEFORE YOU READ	GRIZZLY BEARS	AFTER YOU READ
	What do grizzly bears do in the winter?	
	How long do grizzly bears live?	
	Why do people kill grizzly bears?	

The Bear Man

GRIZZLY BEARS CAN BE VERY dangerous to people. People can be dangerous to grizzly bears, too. Some people kill them for fur or for food.

5 Grizzly bears can live for about 30 years. But **half** of them die before they are five years old.

Grizzly bears **hibernate** every winter. They sleep for a long time. They
10 don't wake up or eat for **several** months. When they wake up in the spring, the grizzlies are **in danger** again. But in Alaska, in the U.S., the grizzly bears are not alone. Timothy
15 Treadwell is there to protect them. He sleeps in a tent near the bears and bathes in a river with them, too. People do not **hurt** the bears when Timothy is with them.

20 Timothy went to Alaska for the first time about 12 years ago. He loved the beauty of the land and the animals. But he learned that people kill many grizzly bears every year. Timothy wanted to
25 protect the grizzly bears. Timothy wants to keep the bears safe from danger, so he lives with the bears for four to five months every year.

Timothy has lived with the grizzlies
30 every spring for about 12 years. Some bears are now his friends. He gave them names. His friend Booble sometimes gives him fish. His friend Lazy sleeps near his tent every night.
35 Every winter, Timothy **returns** to his home in California when the bears hibernate. Then he **teaches** children and adults about his friends in Alaska.

1. **Main Idea.** What is the most important idea of the story? Fill in the bubble.

(A) Grizzly bears can live for 30 years.

(B) Timothy Treadwell lives with grizzly bears to protect them.

(C) Timothy Treadwell went to Alaska 12 years ago.

2. **Just the Facts.** Check (✓) **True or False. If a sentence is false, change it to make it true.**

	True	False
1. Grizzly bears can live for about 50 years. Grizzly bears can live for about 30 years.	☐	✔
2. Timothy wants to hurt the bears.	☐	☐
3. Timothy sleeps in a river near the bears.	☐	☐
4. He lives with the bears for four or five months every year.	☐	☐
5. Grizzly bears hibernate in the spring.	☐	☐
6. Timothy teaches people about the land in Alaska.	☐	☐
7. Timothy lives in California in the winter.	☐	☐

3. **Learn New Words.** Circle the words that have the same meaning as the underlined words.

1. Grizzly bears hibernate in the winter. They don't wake up to eat or drink.
(sleep for a long time)   look for food

2. They don't wake up for several months. They sleep all winter.
one or two   many

3. The grizzlies are in danger again in the spring. People try to kill them.
not safe   alone

4. But half of all grizzly bears die before they are five years old.
25%   50%

5. People do not hurt the bears when Timothy is with them. Timothy keeps them safe.
protect   are not dangerous to

4. Complete the Paragraph. Use the words below to complete the paragraph.

~~gives~~   returns   sleeps   teaches

Some bears are Timothy's friends. Booble (1) _____gives_____ him fish to eat.
Lazy (2) _____ near his tent every night. Every winter, Timothy
(3) _____ to his home in California. He (4) _____ children and
adults about his friends in Alaska.

5. Think It Over. With a partner, write each sentence on the correct side of the chart.

~~Timothy sleeps in a tent in Alaska.~~   Timothy lives in California.
The grizzly bears hibernate.   The bears do not eat for several months.
Timothy teaches people about grizzlies.   Some people try to kill the grizzlies.
Timothy protects bears.   Booble gives some fish to Timothy.

IN THE SPRING	IN THE WINTER
Timothy sleeps in a tent in Alaska.	

6. Write It Down. Write a paragraph about grizzly bears.

_____ Grizzly bears can live for about 30 years. _____

_____

_____

7. Talk It Over. Timothy does not sleep with the bears when they hibernate. Why not? Write some ideas below. Then share your ideas with a partner.

_____

_____

CHAPTER 14

The Tree Lady

Before You Read. Look at the picture and read the title of the story.

1. **Circle your answers and write them on the lines.**

   This woman is _____ in a tree.   standing   working

   She wants to _____ the tree.   protect   hurt

   Some people want to cut down this tree for _____.   food   wood

2. **Circle your answer.**

   Are trees important?   Yes   No

The Tree Lady

JULIA BUTTERFLY HILL WAS upset. A large company **cut down** big redwood trees in a forest in California, in the U.S. The company cut down several trees for wood. Redwood trees are the tallest trees in the world and they are very old. Julia believes that these trees are very important to the Earth because they are so old. She didn't want the company to cut down the trees. The trees were in danger, and she wanted to protect them. So one day, Julia Butterfly Hill **climbed** a tall tree in that forest and lived in it.

Julia's tree is 180 feet (about 55 meters) tall and over 1,000 years old. Julia called her tree Luna. She lived in the tree for more than two years! The company wanted Julia to come down. She didn't want to come down. She didn't want the company to cut down Luna and the other trees. Her friends agreed. They **helped** her. They brought food, water, and blankets to her.

The weather was often very cold and windy. But Julia did not come down. Many people knew about Julia. They also agreed with her. They believed that the trees were very important. Television reporters came to speak to her. Her story was in newspapers, too.

Finally, after two years, the company agreed. It will not cut down Luna or the other trees nearby. Julia Butterfly Hill climbed down from the redwood. She was tired, dirty, and hungry. But she was happy.

---

1. **Main Idea.** What is the most important idea of the story? Fill in the bubble.

(A) Some companies cut down trees for wood.

(B) Julia Butterfly Hill wanted to protect the redwood trees.

(C) Many newspapers wrote stories about Julia Butterfly Hill.

2. **Just the Facts.** Underline the correct answers. Write them on the lines.

1. ____A company____ wanted to cut down redwood trees.
   Julia   A company

2. Redwood trees are the _____ trees in the world.
                          oldest   tallest

3. _____ believes redwood trees are important to the Earth.
   Julia   The company

4. Julia's friends _____ with her.
                    agreed   lived

5. _____ wanted Julia to come down from the tree.
   Her friends   The company

3. **Learn New Words.** Circle the correct words. Write them on the lines.

1. Julia Butterfly Hill ____was upset____ with a large company.
   (was upset)   agreed

2. It cut down redwood trees for _____.
                                 fun   wood

3. So Julia _____ a redwood tree and lived in it.
            climbed   cut down

4. She lived in Luna for two years because she didn't want the company to
   _____ the tree.
   climb   cut down

5. Her friends _____ her. They brought food, clothes, and water.
               believed   helped

6. After two years, the company _____ agreed. It will not cut down the
   redwood trees.   finally   never

4. **Write It Down.** Now write the sentences in Activity 3 as a paragraph.

Julia Butterfly Hill was upset with a large company.

_____

_____

_____

_____

_____

5. **Finish the Sentences.** With a partner, draw lines from the words on the left to the words on the right to complete the sentences. Then write the sentences below.

1. The company wanted to cut Luna down because   **a.** for two years.
2. Redwood trees are   **b.** very old and very tall.
3. Julia climbed the tree because   **c.** it wanted wood.
4. Julia lived in the tree   **d.** won't cut down the trees.
5. Now the company   **e.** she wanted to protect it.

1. The company wanted to cut Luna down because it wanted wood.

2. _____

3. _____

4. _____

5. _____

6. **Talk It Over.** These five words describe Julia Butterfly Hill in the story: **upset, tired, dirty, hungry,** and **happy.** Talk about these words with a partner. Then, choose three of them and write sentences about Julia. Share your sentences with your partner.

Example: Julia was upset because a large company cut down redwood trees.

1. Julia was _____ because _____
2. Julia was _____ because _____
3. Julia was _____ because _____

Activity Menu

1. **Tie It Together.** Look at the words below. Which words go with Chapter 13? Chapter 14? Both? With a partner, write them in the diagram below.

~~Alaska~~	climb	food	~~protect~~	tent
bears	company	forest	safe	trees
blankets	~~cut down~~	friends	sleep	winter
California	danger	hibernate	spring	wood

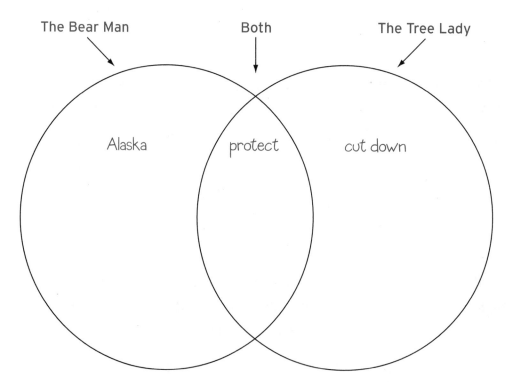

The Bear Man   Both   The Tree Lady

Alaska   protect   cut down

2. **Write It Down.** Which person is more unusual, Timothy Treadwell or Julia Butterfly Hill? Circle your answer and write it on the line. Then write your reason on the next line. Share your answer with a partner.

1. _____ is more unusual.

     Timothy Treadwell   Julia Butterfly Hill

2. I think this person is more unusual because _____

_____

3. **Take a Survey.** Share your answers from Activity 2 with a group. Take a class survey. Count the answers and put the numbers in the chart.

STATEMENTS	NUMBER OF STUDENTS
Timothy Treadwell is more unusual.	
Julia Butterfly Hill is more unusual.	

4. **Just for Fun.** With a partner, use the clues in the box to complete the puzzle.

Clues

Across
2. sleep many months
4. not safe
5. go up
8. after a long time
9. keep something safe

Down
1. many
3. before spring
6. not clean
7. 50%

5. **Go Online.** Use an Internet search engine like Google and type in "grizzly bears." What do they eat? Write your answer on the line. Share it with your classmates.

Grizzly bears eat _____

CHAPTER 15

Ghost Month

Before You Read. Look at the picture and read the title of the story.

1. **Choose the correct word and write it on the line.**

   eat   feast   food

   This is a _____.

   There is a lot of _____ on the table.

   People _____ at a feast.

2. **Circle your answer or write it on the line. Share your answers with your classmates.**

   Did you ever go to a feast?   Yes   No

   Why do people have feasts? _____

Ghost Month

WEI-YI CHENG IS VERY BUSY. SHE IS **preparing** wonderful food for a special day. She is cooking a lot of different food: rice, vegetables, fish,
5 and sweet desserts. This will be a **delicious** feast. All around Taiwan, Wei-Yi's friends and family are also cooking feasts. They cook all kinds of delicious food, too. They also prepare beautiful
10 clothing for the visitors. They all want to be ready for this special day. But the visitors are not people. They are **ghosts**!

In Taiwan, and in many other
15 countries in Asia, people celebrate Ghost Month. This is a very old **tradition**. Ghost Month is the seventh month of the Chinese calendar. People
20 believe that ghosts walk the Earth at that time. Ghosts are people who died. People want the ghosts to be happy. Then the ghosts will not hurt people. On the first day of Ghost Month, Wei-Yi Cheng and many others have a feast for
25 all the ghosts. They light candles and play music for the ghosts at the start of Ghost Month, too.

During Ghost Month, many Taiwanese do not get married or buy
30 new houses. They do not start new **businesses** or go swimming at this time. It is bad luck to do these things in Ghost Month. At the end of Ghost Month, it's time for the ghosts to leave.
35 Wei-Yi prepares another feast for the ghosts. She puts the food outside her home this time. The ghosts are happy, and the people feel safe again.

1. **Main Idea.** What is the most important idea of the story? Fill in the bubble.

- (A) Many people do not go swimming in Ghost Month.
- (B) Wei-Yi and many others prepare feasts for ghosts.
- (C) People celebrate Ghost Month in Asia.

2. Just the Facts. Circle the correct answers. Write them on the lines.

1. Wei-Yi prepares a feast on ____the first day____ of Ghost Month.
   (the first day)   the seventh day

2. People who died are _____.
   visitors   ghosts

3. Ghost Month is the seventh month of the Chinese _____.
   feast   calendar

4. It is bad luck to _____ in Ghost Month.
   prepare a feast   get married

5. The ghosts leave at the _____ of Ghost Month.
   end   beginning

3. Learn New Words. Circle the words that have the same meaning as the underlined words.

1. Wei-Yi Cheng is <u>preparing</u> wonderful food for a special day.
   eating   (making)

2. This feast will <u>be delicious</u>. Everyone will enjoy the food.
   taste very good   be different

3. Wei-Yi's friends cook <u>all kinds of</u> delicious foods: rice, vegetables, fish, and desserts.
   some   many different

4. People believe that <u>ghosts</u> walk the Earth in Ghost Month.
   visitors   people who died

5. Ghost Month is an old <u>tradition</u> in Taiwan. Many people in Asia celebrate Ghost Month.
   custom   feast

6. People light candles and play music for the ghosts <u>at the start of</u> Ghost Month. They also have a feast on the first day.
   before   in the beginning of

4. Complete the Paragraph. Use the words below to complete the paragraph.

bad luck   businesses   houses   ~~married~~   swimming

During Ghost Month, many Taiwanese do not get (1) _____married_____. They do not
buy new (2) _____. They stay in their old ones. They do not start new
(3) _____ like restaurants or stores. Many people do not go (4) _____
at this time. It is (5) _____ to do these things in Ghost Month.

5. Finish the Sentences. Draw lines from the words on the left to the words on the right to complete the sentences. Then write the sentences below.

1. Ghost Month is the month
2. People do not get married then
3. People prepare feasts for the ghosts
4. People put food outside on the last day

a. because it is bad luck.
b. because they want the ghosts to leave.
c. when ghosts walk the Earth.
d. because they want the ghosts to be happy.

1. _Ghost Month is the month when ghosts walk the Earth._
2. _____
3. _____
4. _____

6. Write It Down. Look at the story again. Write two or three sentences about Wei-Yi Cheng.

Wei-Yi Cheng prepares wonderful food for Ghost Month.
_____
_____

7. Talk It Over. People don't go swimming in Ghost Month in Taiwan. It is bad luck. What do you think is bad luck? Share your answers with your classmates.

BAD LUCK

CHAPTER 16

A Modern Tradition

Before You Read. Look at the picture and read the title of the story.

1. **Circle your answers and write them on the lines.**

   This woman is a _____.

   People can _____ her about the future.

teacher	fortune-teller
tell	ask

2. **Write two questions you have about your future.**

   _____

   _____

A Modern Tradition

YONG SOOK LIM **GRADUATED** FROM college a month ago. She lives in Seoul, Korea. She has many questions about her future, like most young
5 people. Will she find a good job? Will she be **successful**? Will she have a family someday? At the start of the new year, many Koreans go to fortune-tellers. This is called *chom*.
10 This tradition is **ancient** in Korea. It is more than 4,000 years old. Many people believe fortune-tellers know the **future**. There are a lot of fortune-tellers in Seoul. They are in **modern**
15 coffee shops all around the city. But *chom* is not **cheap**. It costs about U.S. $25.00.

Many young people, like Yong Sook, don't like to go to coffee shops
20 to see fortune-tellers. Sometimes they are **embarrassed**. Sometimes it is too **expensive** for them. Now they can go to fortune-tellers on the Internet. These fortune-tellers are
25 usually free or very cheap. When Yong Sook has a question about her future, she goes to a *chom* Web site. She types her birth date—the month, day, year, and hour of her birth—on
30 the computer. These four important numbers are called *saju*. The fortune-teller uses this information to tell the future.

Many young Koreans go to
35 Internet fortune-tellers every week. Some say it is just for fun. It makes them feel happy. *Chom* is a very old tradition in Korea. But Yong Sook and her friends can use this ancient
40 tradition in a modern way.

1. **Main Idea.** What is the most important idea of the story? Fill in the bubble.

(A) Many young Koreans go to coffee shops in Seoul.

(B) Many young Koreans go to fortune-tellers online.

(C) Yong Sook feels happy when she goes online.

2. Just the Facts. Check (✓) True or False. If a sentence is false, change it to make it true.

	True	False
1. Many people believe fortune-tellers know the past. <u>Many people believe fortune-tellers know the future.</u>	☐	✔
2. Yong Sook has many questions about her future.	☐	☐
3. Online fortune-tellers are usually expensive.	☐	☐
4. *Chom* is a new tradition in Korea.	☐	☐
5. Some people are embarrassed to go to fortune-tellers in coffee shops.	☐	☐

3. Learn New Words. Circle the words that have the same meaning as the underlined words.

1. Yong Sook wants to have a family <u>someday</u>. But she wants to find a good job first.

        now   (in the future)

2. <u>At the start of</u> the new year, many Koreans go to fortune-tellers. Fortune-tellers are very

The day before   In the beginning of

busy the first month of the year.

3. Yong Sook Lim <u>graduated from</u> college a month ago. Now she wants to find a job.

        started   finished

4. Some Koreans go to Internet *chom* <u>just</u> for fun. They don't go for other reasons.

        only   maybe

4. Complete the Paragraph. Use the words below to complete the sentences.

~~ancient~~   cheap   embarrassed   expensive   modern   successful

Korean fortune-telling is over 4,000 years old. This (1) ____ancient____ tradition is called *chom*. Fortune-telling is an old and ancient tradition, but today, fortune-tellers are in (2) _____ coffee shops in Seoul. But *chom* is (3) _____. It costs about U.S. $25.00. Internet *chom* is sometimes free, or it is very (4) _____. Yong Sook does not want to go to a traditional fortune-teller because she is (5) _____. But she has questions about her future. Will she be (6) _____? Now Yong Sook can ask questions on a *chom* Web site.

5. Talk It Over. Some fortune-tellers use birth dates and times to tell the future. This is *saju*. What other things do fortune-tellers use to tell the future? Make a list and share it with your classmates.

FORTUNE-TELLING	
birth dates and times (saju)	

6. Take a Survey. Ask your classmates the question below. Count their answers and put the numbers on the chart.

QUESTION	YES	NO
Do you think fortune-tellers know the future?		

7. Write It Down. Complete the sentence below.

I (want/don't want) to go to a fortune-teller because _____

_____

Activity Menu

1. **Tie It Together.** Write each word in the correct point on the star below. Then add more words from Chapters 15 and 16. Share your work with a partner.

Asia	feast	future	prepare	Taiwan
cook	fortune-tellers	happy	Seoul	tradition
embarrassed	~~friends~~	Korea	swimming	visitors

More words:

_____   _____   _____   _____

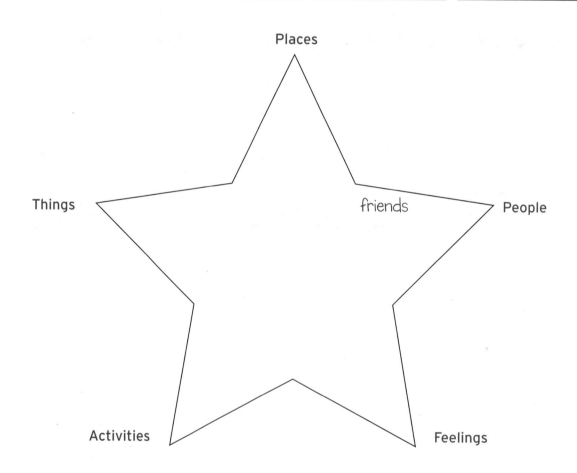

Places

Things

friends

People

Activities

Feelings

2. **Talk It Over.** Ghost Month and fortune-telling are traditions. What are some other traditions? Share your ideas with your classmates. Then complete the chart.

NAME	COUNTRY	TRADITION
Yong Sook	Korea	fortune-telling

3. **Write It Down.** Choose one tradition from Activity 2. Write two to three sentences about it.

Example: Fortune-telling is a tradition in Korea. Fortune-tellers use birth dates...

_____

_____

_____

4. **Just for Fun.** Find and circle these words in the puzzle below.

P	Q	T	N	E	I	C	N	A	S
O	D	H	G	X	C	M	A	U	J
P	E	L	A	P	E	H	C	F	W
U	L	S	G	E	L	C	E	E	G
L	I	A	H	N	E	O	B	A	L
A	C	F	O	S	B	Q	J	S	P
R	I	X	S	I	R	P	W	T	Z
E	O	F	T	V	A	A	A	J	R
T	U	U	G	E	T	P	F	Y	P
L	S	B	N	R	E	D	O	M	A

Word List

ancient
celebrate
cheap
delicious
expensive
feast
ghost
modern
~~popular~~
successful

CHAPTER 17

Smart Refrigerators

Before You Read. Look at the picture and read the title of the story.

1. **Answer the questions. Circle your answers or write them on the lines.**

   What does your refrigerator do? Write two things.

   _____   _____

   Does the refrigerator in the photograph look unusual?   Yes   No

   Why? _____ .

2. **Answer the questions about a smart refrigerator. Circle Yes, No, or Maybe.**

QUESTIONS	ANSWERS		
Does it make ice?	Yes	No	Maybe
Does it order food from the store?	Yes	No	Maybe
Does it keep food cold?	Yes	No	Maybe
Does it connect to the Internet?	Yes	No	Maybe

Smart Refrigerators

WHAT DOES YOUR REFRIGERATOR DO? It keeps your food cold. It makes ice. It freezes food. But in the future, refrigerators may do much more. They
5 may tell you what food is inside. They may tell you what food you need. They may shop for you, too!

Some companies are making online refrigerators. These refrigerators have
10 a computer screen on the door. The computer is connected to your supermarket through the Internet. This can be very **useful**. For example, when you finish your orange juice, you can
15 **put** the **empty** juice carton near the computer screen. The computer reads the bar code on the juice carton. Then it **orders** more orange juice from the supermarket. You can also use the
20 computer screen to order other things from the supermarket. The computer screen has a list of things that are in the store. You can choose what you need. The supermarket will **deliver** your
25 food to your home.

Companies are making other "smart" appliances, too. There is a new kind of microwave oven. It has a computer memory. It can remember
30 365 different recipes. There is also a smart mixer. It can remember recipes, too. It can also measure ingredients for you!

Of course, sometimes these smart
35 appliances can break. When they do, they tell you. And then they can call someone to fix them, too!

1. **Main Idea.** **What is the most important idea of the story? Fill in the bubble.**

(A) Online refrigerators have a computer screen on the door.

(B) Smart appliances, like online refrigerators, can be very helpful.

(C) Refrigerators of the future may order food from the supermarket.

2. **Just the Facts.** **Read the sentences about smart refrigerators. Check (✓) True or False.**

	True	False
1. They can show you a list of food in the supermarket.	✔	
2. They can clean themselves.		
3. They can cook for you.		
4. They can order food from the supermarket.		
5. They can keep food cold.		
6. They can play music.		
7. They can read bar codes on food.		
8. They can remember recipes.		

3. **Learn New Words.** **Choose the correct words. Circle your answers and write them on the lines.**

1. Online refrigerators can be very _____useful_____. They can do a lot of helpful things.
   empty (useful)

2. Microwave ovens will _____ 365 recipes. They will have good memories.
   remember   order

3. The refrigerator connects to the supermarket through the _____.
   oven   Internet

4. When you finish the juice, the carton is _____.
   empty   useful

4. Complete the Paragraph. Use the words below to complete the paragraph.

| choose | delivers | ~~finish~~ | orders | put | reads |

First, you (1) _____finish_____ your orange juice. Then you (2) _____
the empty juice carton near the computer screen. The computer (3) _____
the bar code on the juice carton. It (4) _____ more orange juice from the
supermarket. You can (5) _____ other things, too. Then the supermarket
(6) _____ your food to your home.

5. Think It Over. Look at the chart below. Write two sentences for each appliance:
one sentence that describes it now, and one sentence that describes it in the future.

	REFRIGERATOR	MICROWAVE	MIXER
Now	It keeps food cold and makes ice.		
In the future			

6. Write It Down. It is now the year 2050. Write three to four sentences about an
appliance that you use often. How do you use it?

I use my _____ often. It can _____

_____

_____

7. Talk It Over. Read the question below. With a partner, check (✓) **Yes** or **No** for each
choice. Add two more choices. Share your answers with your classmates.

WHO NEEDS AN ONLINE REFRIGERATOR?	YES	NO
people who have a car		
people who like to walk to the store		
people who are sick		
people who are very busy		

CHAPTER 18

The Home of the Future

Before You Read. Look at the picture and read the title of the story.

1. **Circle your answers and write them on the lines.**

   The woman with the baby is _____ the house.   inside   outside

   The man watching TV is _____ the house.   inside   outside

   The man _____ see the woman.   can   can't

2. **Read the sentences about homes of the future. Check your answers on the left. After you read the story, check your answers on the right.**

BEFORE YOU READ		THE HOME OF THE FUTURE	AFTER YOU READ	
AGREE	DISAGREE		AGREE	DISAGREE
		It opens the door for you.		
		It turns on lights for you.		
		It turns on music for you.		

The Home of the Future

WHEN DAN GREEN COMES HOME from work, he doesn't need a key to open his front door. As he walks up to the front of his house, the door
5 opens. The lights turn on **inside**. His favorite music starts to play. His dinner is ready in the oven. But no one is home. What's happening? This is the home of the future! Right now,
10 Dan Green is the only person who has a home like this. He is a scientist. But in about 25 years, many people will have homes like Dan's. His home does not look different on the **outside**. But
15 inside it is very different.

Computers **control** this house of the future. For example, Dan is watching television when the doorbell rings. The TV is a computer. When
20 Dan presses a button on the TV remote control, he can see a picture of his visitor on the screen. He can also use the remote control to open or close the door. Dan can watch TV
25 and **answer** the door at the same time. Computers control the windows and the temperature, too. The computers remember the right temperature for Dan.

30 When Dan goes to sleep at night, an electric blanket is already warm in his bed. It **turns on** a half hour before Dan goes to bed. In the morning, an alarm clock wakes Dan up. But it also
35 **turns off** the electric blanket. Then it turns on the coffee maker. Dan's coffee is ready before he is. This is very useful! Dan's home protects him, too. It knows when someone comes
40 into his house. It can tell Dan when there is a fire. Soon there may be a lot of these homes. They will keep all of us **comfortable** and safe.

---

1. **Main Idea.** **What is the most important idea of the story? Fill in the bubble.**

(A) Dan Green's alarm clock turns on his coffee maker.

(B) Homes of the future will keep us safe.

(C) Computers will control homes in the future.

2. Just the Facts. Check (✓) True or False. If a sentence is false, change it to make it true.

	True	False
1. Dan Green needs a key to open his front door.	☐	✔

Dan Green doesn't need a key to open his front door.

	True	False
2. Today there are a lot of homes of the future.	☐	☐
_____		
3. Homes of the future do not look different on the inside.	☐	☐
_____		
4. Computers control the appliances.	☐	☐
_____		
5. Dan turns on the coffee maker when he gets up.	☐	☐
_____		

3. Learn New Words. Choose the correct words. Write them on the lines.

~~answer~~   comfortable   control   inside   presses

1. Dan can watch TV and _____answer_____ the door at the same time.

2. The house does not look different on the outside. But _____ it is very different.

3. Computers _____ everything in this house of the future, such as the temperature, the windows, and the alarm clock.

4. Dan _____ a button on the remote control to see a picture of his visitor.

5. We will have everything we need in the homes of the future. The homes will keep us _____ and safe.

4. Complete the Paragraph. Use the phrases below to complete the paragraph. Use each phrase more than once.

turns on   turns off

An electric blanket (1) _____turns on_____ a half hour before Dan goes to bed. In the morning, an alarm clock (2) _____ the electric blanket. Then it (3) _____ the coffee maker. When Dan leaves the house, the music (4) _____.

5. **Think It Over.** The home of the future can do many useful things. Look at the reading. Write some things on the chart below. Share your answers with your classmates.

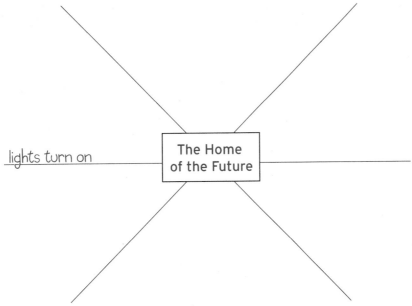

lights turn on —— The Home of the Future

6. **Write It Down.** Choose one thing from Activity 5. Write a paragraph about why it is useful.

Example: In the home of the future, the lights turn on when you come home. This is helpful because...

_____

_____

_____

_____

_____

7. **Talk It Over.** What other things do you think the homes of the future may do? Share your ideas with a group. Then write them here:

WHAT DO YOU THINK THE HOMES OF THE FUTURE MAY DO?		

Activity Menu

1. **Tie It Together.** Dan Green lives in the home of the future. He has an online refrigerator, too. Write sentences about a day in his home. Share your sentences with a partner.

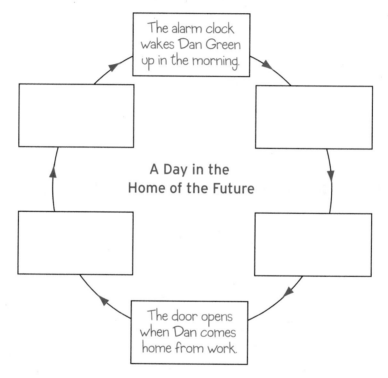

The alarm clock wakes Dan Green up in the morning.

A Day in the Home of the Future

The door opens when Dan comes home from work.

2. **Talk It Over.** Do you want to live in a home of the future? Why or why not? Share your reasons with a group. Then write them here:

I (want/don't want) to live in a home of the future because _____

_____

3. **Write It Down.** Write a paragraph about your day in your home of the future. Use ideas from the stories in Chapters 17 and 18. You may use different ideas, too.

When I wake up, _____

_____

_____

_____

4. Just for Fun. With a partner, unscramble these new words. Then use the letters in the circles to make a word in the boxes below.

RERARGOTFERI — R [ ][ ][(○)][ ][ ][ ][ ][ ]

VAWECROIM VONE — M [ ][ ][ ][ ][(○)][ ] [O][ ][ ]

FEFOEC ERAKM — C [ ][ ][ ][ ][M][(○)][ ][ ]

MALRA CLKCO — A [ ][ ][ ][(C)][ ][ ][ ]

SOELVNITEI — T [(○)][(○)][ ][ ][(○)][ ][(○)]

[A][P][P][ ][ ][ ][ ][ ][ ]

5. Take a Survey. What is the most important appliance for you today? What was the most important appliance for your parents 20 years ago? Complete the chart with a group. Then compare it with another group's chart.

NAME	MOST IMPORTANT APPLIANCE FOR YOU TODAY	MOST IMPORTANT APPLIANCE FOR YOUR PARENTS 20 YEARS AGO

CHAPTER 19

Tornado Warning!

Before You Read. Look at the pictures and read the title of the story.

1. **Circle your answers and write them on the lines.**

   This is a _____.   tornado   earthquake

   It is very _____.   safe   dangerous

   It _____ hurt you.   can't   can

2. **Write your answers on the lines.**

   Did you ever see a tornado? _____

   Where did you see it? _____

Tornado Warning!

NANCY BOSE WAS ASLEEP WHEN A terrible tornado hit her town many years ago. Her parents quickly woke her up. They all ran down to the basement.
5 The noise was terrible. The strong winds broke the basement windows. Nancy and her family were safe, but Nancy was **terrified**. After the tornado, or twister, was gone, they all went outside and
10 looked around. Many of the houses were gone. Nancy was only five years old. But she will never forget that terrible day.

From that day on, Nancy was afraid of tornados. Her parents wanted to help
15 her. They taught her many things about the weather. They taught her a lot about tornados. After a while, she wasn't afraid of tornados anymore. She thought tornados were **fascinating**!
20 Nancy **grew up**, but she still loved tornados. She often read about them on the Internet. She also liked to talk about them. Nancy met a group of people online. They loved tornados, too. Now Nancy and
25 her new friends study tornados together. Every year, they **follow** tornados to learn more about them. They use the Internet, cell phones, and a weather computer to help them find tornados. They want to
30 know when a tornado will hit. Then they can tell people about the twister **ahead of time.** They can **warn** people before it happens. Nancy and her group also teach other people how to know when a twister
35 will hit.

Nancy Bose and her group are always very careful. Tornados are very dangerous, but the group knows how to stay safe. Now they can help other
40 people stay safe, too.

---

1. **Main Idea.** What is the most important idea of the story? Fill in the bubble

- (A) Nancy Bose was five years old when a tornado hit her town.
- (B) Nancy Bose studies and teaches others about tornados.
- (C) A group uses a weather computer to find tornados.

2. Learn New Words. Circle the words that have the same meaning as the underlined words.

1. The tornado was very loud. The basement windows broke, and Nancy was <u>terrified</u>.

   very careful   (very afraid)

2. Nancy loved to learn about tornados. She thought they were <u>fascinating</u>.

   very interesting   very dangerous

3. The people in Nancy's group use cell phones, the Internet, and a weather computer. It tells them about the twister <u>ahead of time</u>.

   after it happens   before it happens

4. The group knows when a tornado is coming. They can <u>warn people</u>.

   tell people to be careful   tell people to use cell phones

5. When she was young, Nancy learned about tornados from her parents. But she read about tornados on the Internet when she <u>grew up</u>.

   woke up   got older

3. Just the Facts. Circle the correct words. Write your answers on the lines.

a. Nancy's group knows when a tornado will hit _____ahead of time_____.

   after it happens   (ahead of time)

b. She learned about tornados and wasn't afraid _____.

   anymore   for a little while

c. Nancy Bose was only five years old when a tornado hit her _____.

   town   basement

d. So the group can _____ before a tornado happens.

   meet people online   warn people

e. Now Nancy and her friends _____ tornados.

   follow   are afraid of

f. The tornado was terrible, and Nancy was afraid _____.

   from that day on   for a little while

g. Her parents _____ her about the weather.

   warned   taught

4. **What Happened First?** Put the sentences from Activity 3 in the correct order. Then, write them as a paragraph below.

a. _____ b. _____ c. ___1___ d. _____ e. _____ f. _____ g. _____

_____Nancy Bose was only five years old when a tornado hit her town._____

_____

_____

_____

_____

_____

5. **Finish the Sentences.** With a partner, draw lines from the words on the left to the words on the right to complete the sentences.

1. Nancy still loved tornados
2. The group wants to know
3. Many houses were gone
4. Nancy wasn't afraid of tornados
5. The group can warn people about a tornado

a. after the tornado hit.
b. after she learned about them.
c. when she grew up.
d. ahead of time.
e. when a tornado will hit.

6. **Talk It Over.** Nancy Bose was afraid of tornados when she was a child. After she learned about tornados, she wasn't afraid anymore. Answer the questions below. Share your answers with your classmates.

When you were a child, what were you afraid of? _____

Are you afraid of this now? (Circle your answer.)   Yes   No

Why or why not? _____

7. **Write It Down.** You are Nancy Bose. What happened when the tornado hit your town? Write a paragraph about it.

_____A tornado hit my town when I was five years old._____

_____

_____

_____

_____

CHAPTER 20

The Highest Peak

Before You Read. Look at the picture and read the title of the story.

1. **Circle your answers and write them on the lines.**

   These people are on a _____.   mountain   street

   One man is sitting on a machine because he _____. can't see   can't walk

2. **Answer the questions. Write your answers on the chart.**

QUESTIONS	ANSWERS
Do you climb mountains?	
Why do some people climb mountains?	
What are some mountains that people climb?	

The Highest Peak

PETE RIEKE (PRONOUNCED REE-KEE) reached the top of Mount Rainier in Washington, in the U.S. He climbed to the **peak** in ten days. The
5 temperature was freezing. The winds were very strong. But Pete Rieke was happy. Mount Rainier is the tallest mountain in Washington. It is also the most difficult to climb. Every year,
10 about 11,000 people try to climb it. Only about 50% are successful. Pete can not walk, but he climbed Mount Rainier.

Pete Rieke first climbed a
15 mountain when he was 15 years old. From that day on, he loved it! He grew up and climbed mountains all over the United States. But he had a **terrible** accident when he was 40
20 years old. He fell when he was climbing. The doctors said he could not walk anymore. But Pete wanted to climb again. It was his **dream**. He and his friends decided to make
25 something to help Pete climb. They used ice skates, bicycle parts, and other things. They worked hard. In fact, they worked for four years! But finally they made a "snow pod." Pete
30 can sit in it and use his arms to move it. The snow pod helped Pete climb mountains again. This was a great **success** for Pete, and for his friends, too.
35 Pete Rieke tried to climb Mount Rainier in the snow pod three times. The first two times, the weather was too terrible. He had to stop climbing. He was successful on his third try.
40 But Pete did not do it **alone**. He had many friends to help him get to the top.

---

1. **Main Idea.** What is the most important idea of the story? Fill in the bubble.

(A) Mount Rainier is the tallest mountain in Washington.

(B) Pete Rieke had a terrible mountain climbing accident and can't climb anymore.

(C) Pete Rieke can't walk, but he has a snow pod to help him climb mountains.

2. Learn New Words. Choose the correct words. Write them on the lines.

alone   dream   ~~peak~~   success   terrible

1. Pete Rieke reached the top of the mountain. He climbed to the _____peak_____ in ten days.

2. Pete did not climb the mountain the first two times. The weather was too _____.

3. Pete wanted to climb again after his accident. It was his _____.

4. Many friends helped Pete. He did not climb the mountain _____.

5. He finally climbed the mountain. This was a great _____ for Pete.

3. Just the Facts. Circle the correct answers and write them on the lines.

a. Pete and his friends made a snow pod to help him _____climb_____.
   (climb)   walk

b. Pete Rieke _____ climbed a mountain when he was 15 years old.
   first   finally

c. Pete Rieke _____ climbed Mount Rainier on his third try.
   first   finally

d. Pete could not _____, but he always knew that he would climb again.
   walk   work

e. He sits in it and _____.
   his friends push him   moves it with his arms

f. He had a terrible accident when he was _____ years old.
   40   15

4. **What Happened First?** With a partner, put the sentences in Activity 3 in the correct order. Then write them below as a paragraph.

a. _____ b. __*1*__ c. _____ d. _____ e. _____ f. _____

_____Pete Rieke first climbed a mountain when he was 15 years old._____

_____

_____

_____

_____

_____

5. **Write It Down.** Look at the story again. Write three to four sentences about Mount Rainier.

Mount Rainier is in Washington._____

_____

_____

_____

6. **Find the Answers.** Read the questions. Find the answers in the story.

1. How many people climb to the top of Mount Rainier every year?

_____

2. How does the snow pod work?

_____

3. Why didn't Pete climb to the top of Mount Rainier the first two times?

_____

7. **Talk It Over.** Pete Rieke's dream was to climb mountains again. What is your dream? Complete the sentences. Share your answers with your classmates.

My dream is to _____

This is my dream because _____

To do this, I need _____

Activity Menu

CHAPTERS 19 AND 20

1. **Tie It Together.** Look at the words below. Which words go with Chapter 19? Chapter 20? Both? With a partner, write them in the diagram below. Then add some more words from the chapters.

accident	dream	Internet	success	weather
~~climb~~	fascinating	mountain	terrified	winds
~~dangerous~~	friends	peak	~~tornado~~	

More words:

_____   _____   _____   _____

Tornado Warning!   Both   The Highest Peak

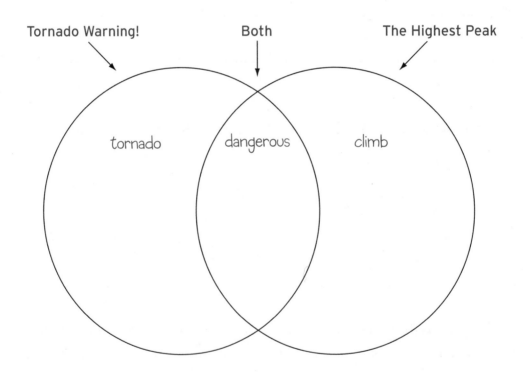

tornado   dangerous   climb

2. **Talk It Over.** Pete Rieke enjoys mountain climbing. Nancy Bose enjoys studying tornados. What do you like to do in your free time? Complete the sentence, then share your answer with your classmates.

In my free time I like to _____

_____

3. Write It Down. Complete the chart below with a partner.

PERSON	NANCY BOSE	PETE RIEKE
Problem	She was afraid of tornados.	
Solution		
Result		Now he can climb mountains.

4. Just for Fun. With a partner, use the clues in the box to complete the puzzle.

Clues

Across
1. ~~not safe~~
4. very interesting
6. in the end
8. very afraid
9. tornado
10. the top of a mountain

Down
2. before something happens (three words)
3. not easy
5. without friends
7. not alone

5. Go Online. What is the highest mountain in North America? How high is it?
Use an Internet search engine like Google and type in "highest peak in North America." Complete the sentences.

The highest mountain in North America is _____

It is _____ high.

SKILLS INDEX

READING
Chapter Topics
animals: 42, 46, 56, 62
customs and traditions: 56, 72, 76
education: 32, 36, 62
entertainment: 52, 56, 76
environment and weather: 66, 92
friendship: 2, 6, 16, 96
health: 12, 16, 42
hotels: 52
homes, houses: 86
Internet: 2, 26, 36, 76, 82
marriage: 2, 6
mountain climbing: 96
technology: 26, 82, 86, 96
twins: 2

Comprehension
factual: 4, 8, 9, 11, 14, 15, 18, 19, 24, 25,
28, 31, 34, 35, 38, 39, 40, 44, 45,
48, 50, 54, 58, 59, 60, 62, 64, 65,
68, 69, 74, 75, 78, 84, 88, 89, 94,
95, 98, 99
inferential: 2, 16, 22, 26, 29, 42, 46,
52, 62, 66, 82, 92, 95, 96
main idea: 4, 7, 13, 17, 23, 27, 33, 37, 43,
47, 53, 57, 63, 67, 73, 77, 83, 87, 93,
97

Critical Thinking
5, 10, 20, 26, 29, 31, 34, 35, 39, 45, 49,
50, 54, 59, 60, 62, 65, 66, 69, 70, 72,
82, 85, 89, 95, 96

Group and Partner Work
5, 9, 10, 11, 14, 15, 19, 20, 21, 25, 26, 29,
30, 31, 34, 35, 38, 39, 40, 41, 45, 49,
50, 52, 54, 55, 58, 59, 60, 61, 65,
69, 70, 71, 72, 75, 79, 80, 81, 85, 89,
90, 91, 95, 99, 100, 101

Personal Responses/Opinions
opinions: 5, 9, 10, 12, 15, 16, 19, 21, 25,
29, 35, 39, 45, 50, 51, 55, 56, 58,
60, 70, 76, 79, 81, 90, 95, 99, 100

Pre-reading Activities
2, 6, 12, 16, 22, 26, 32, 36, 42, 46, 52,
56, 62, 66, 72, 76, 82, 86, 92, 96

Reading Through Art
2, 6, 12, 16, 22, 26, 32, 36, 42, 46, 52,
56, 62, 66, 72, 76, 82, 86, 92, 96

Reading Skills
grouping, sorting, classifying: 10, 20,
30, 40, 50, 60, 70, 80, 100
identifying cause and effect: 29, 31,
39, 49, 60, 69, 70
identifying details: 4, 9, 11, 18, 28, 34,
44, 48, 54, 58, 68, 74, 94, 98
sequencing: 4, 95, 99

Taking Surveys
11, 15, 29, 49, 55, 59, 71, 79, 91

Test-taking Skills and Strategies
fill in the blank: 8, 9, 11, 18, 38, 48, 54,
58, 65, 72, 75, 79, 98
fill in bubbles: 4, 7, 13, 17, 23, 27, 33, 37,
43, 47, 53, 57, 63, 67, 73, 77, 84, 87,
93, 97
matching: 14, 18, 25, 35, 45, 69
multiple choice questions: 2, 4, 6, 8,
12, 14, 16, 18, 22, 24, 26, 28, 32, 34,
36, 38, 42, 44, 46, 48, 54, 58, 62,
64, 66, 68, 74, 76, 78, 84, 86, 88,
92, 94, 96, 98

open-ended questions: 6, 9, 10, 12, 15,
16, 19, 20, 21, 25, 26, 29, 31, 35, 36,
39, 44, 45, 49, 51, 55, 58, 59, 60,
65, 69, 70, 71, 72, 75, 76, 79, 81, 82,
85, 89, 90, 91, 95, 96, 99, 100, 101
true/false questions: 24, 64, 78, 84,
88

USING THE INTERNET
Web Search Subjects
colleges: 41
famous twins: 11
grizzly bears: 71
highest mountains: 101
ice hotels: 61
pet therapy: 51

VOCABULARY
introduction of (in story): 3, 7, 13, 17,
23, 27, 33, 37, 43, 47, 53, 57, 63, 67,
73, 77, 83, 87, 93, 97
in context (exercises): 4, 8, 14, 18, 24,
28, 34, 38, 44, 48, 54, 58, 64, 65,
68, 74, 75, 78, 79, 84, 88, 94, 98

WRITING
5, 8, 10, 15, 19, 25, 29, 35, 39, 45, 49,
51, 55, 59, 60, 65, 69, 70, 75, 79,
85, 89, 90, 95, 98, 99, 101

PUZZLES
crosswords: 21, 71, 101
unscrambling sentences: 61
unscrambling words: 31, 41, 91
word searches: 11, 51, 81

VOCABULARY INDEX

Chapter 1
also
both
identical
missed
next door
often

Chapter 2
confused
fell in love
gym
neighbor
propose
spelled
unusual

Chapter 3
laugh
laughter
loud
loudly
quietly
relax
silent
slowly
stress

Chapter 4
depressed
healthy
made
medicine
scientist

Chapter 5
a little while
at night
awake
busy
hard
in the afternoon
in the morning
job
nap
such as

Chapter 6
agree
choose
commute
coworker
crowded
discuss
employee
enjoy
finished
pay for

Chapter 7
agree
almost no
dinner
half an hour
problem
weekend

Chapter 8
exam
helpful
like
near
online
others
take

Chapter 9
bring
calm
car accident
elderly
got better
hospital
patient
pet
stayed
terrible

Chapter 10
allergic
backyard
difficult
memory
miniature
only a few
remember
stare
strong

Chapter 11
build
furniture
made of
melt
temperature
traditional

Chapter 12
especially
gentle
hot spring
near
protect

Chapter 13
give
half
hibernate
hurt
in danger
return
several
sleep
teach

Chapter 14
climbed
cut down
dirty
finally
happy
helped
hungry
tired
upset
wood

Chapter 15
all kinds of
at the start of
bad luck
business
delicious
ghost
house
married
prepare
swimming
tradition

Chapter 16
ancient
at the start of
cheap
embarrassed
expensive
modern
future
graduated
just
someday
successful

Chapter 17
choose
deliver
empty
finish
Internet
order
put
read
remember
useful

Chapter 18
answer (the door)
comfortable
control
inside
outside
press
turn off
turn on

Chapter 19
ahead of time
fascinating
grew up
terrified
warn

Chapter 20
alone
dream
peak
success
terrible